Your Plan For Life

Personal Strategic Planning for Humans

By Case Adams

Your Plan for Life: Personal Strategic Planning
    for Humans
Copyright © 2017 Case Adams
LOGICAL BOOKS
Wilmington, Delaware
http://www.logicalbooks.org
All rights reserved.
Printed in USA
Front cover art

Publishers Cataloging in Publication Data
Adams, Case
Your Plan for Life: Personal Strategic Planning
    for Humans
First Edition
1. Inspiration. 2. Education
Bibliography and References; Index

Paperback ISBN 978-1-936251-52-0
Ebook ISBN 978-1-936251-53-7

NATURAL SOLUTIONS FOR FOOD ALLERGIES AND FOOD INTOLERANCES: Scientifically Proven Remedies for Food Sensitivities

ORAL PROBIOTICS: The Newest Way to Prevent Infection, Boost the Immune System and Fight Disease

PROBIOTICS: Protection Against Infection

PROBIOTICS SIMPLIFIED: How Nature's Tiny Warriors Keep Us Healthy

PROVING HOMEOPATHY: Why Homeopathy Works Only Sometimes

PURE WATER: The Science of Water, Waves, Water Pollution, Water Treatment, Water Therapy and Water Ecology

THE ANCESTORS DIET: Living and Cultured Foods to Extend Life, Prevent Disease and Lose Weight

THE BRAIN, MIND AND UNCONSCIOUS SELF: Unveiling the Ancient Secrets using Science

THE CONSCIOUS ANATOMY: Healing the Real You

THE GLUTEN CURE: Scientifically Proven Natural Solutions to Celiac Disease and Gluten Sensitivities

THE LIVING CLEANSE: Detoxification and Cleansing Using Living Foods and Safe Natural Strategies

THE MEANING OF DREAMS: The Science of Why We Dream, How to Interpret Them and How to Steer Them

THE SCIENCE OF LEAKY GUT SYNDROME: Intestinal Permeability and Digestive Health

TOTAL HARMONIC: The Healing Power of Nature's Elements

Table of Contents

Introduction

Imagine for a moment stepping onto a stage in front of a large audience made up of people who want to hear you speak. Now imagine that you have no written speech, nor have you even made a plan on what you will say.

What will happen? Likely a train wreck. With nothing planned, you might get away with saying something that makes some people laugh. But they may well be laughing at you rather than with you.

Without a plan, you will not be able to fully embrace the opportunity before you: To tell others something that will help them. To tell others something that has meaning and purpose.

In other words, it may well be a waste of time: A waste of your time and a waste of time for those listening in the audience.

How does not having a written speech or plan for what to say relate to having a plan for our lives?

Plenty.

Our life is like giving a speech in front of an audience because each of our lives matter. To us and to others. We will be reflecting upon our lives from time to time, and we will sometimes be our harshest judges.

Others will also see how we live our lives. Others will see, eventually, what our lives meant to us. Others will see what we stand for and who we root for.

Who are others?

They are our children, our mothers, our fathers, our sisters, our brothers, our spouses. Our friends. Our work associates. Our bosses. Our fans. Our customers. Our hosts. Our partners.

Even if we are shy and don't get around much socially, our lives will affect ourselves and others. Even if we are shut-ins or anti-socials, our lives will still affect ourselves and those around us.

How so? Because what others see of our lives will have subtle or significant influences upon them.

Our lives will influence those around us at some point and in some way. In this way, we can say that each of us is an influencer to someone.

Look again at the list of the "others" we may affect at some point in our lives. As an exercise, go through each type, and think of some people in your life who fit within each of those categories. Now in your mind, assemble all of those people from all of the categories and imagine they make up an audience.

But don't stop there. Add to this audience those who you will meet and share times with in the future. Your future friends, associates, customers, partners and so on.

Now add yourself to that audience.

Now imagine that you and all these people are all in the audience and you are the speaker.

The speech is your life. Every part of your speech would be equivalent to an interaction you had with each of those people in the audience at some point in your life.

Now you tell me: Should you prepare for such a speech? Should you make a plan for what you will talk about while you are standing before your audience?

No one in their right mind would say no to such a scenario. No one would think it is appropriate to give such an important a speech without preparation.

Yet many of us will live our lives without a plan.

Doing so would be like getting on a train or an airplane without knowing where the plane or train is going. It would be like a doctor doing surgery on a patient without knowing what disease the patient had, or what the doctor was going to do once he sliced through the skin.

Living life without a plan is living life without constructive purpose.

Some might say this would make life more exciting: To not know what life has in store for us. Live for the moment, they might say. Play it by ear.

But these will happen anyway. Even if we make a plan for life, we will still be presented with so many unexpected things as we journey forward. There will be no shortage of excitement regardless of whether we make a plan.

What a plan will help us avoid is a life that without constructive purpose: A life that is meaningless to us and others. A life that stands for nothing and creates no message for those around us.

Such a life could be—just as a rambling, meaningless speech—a waste of time for us and those who have interacted with us throughout our lifetime.

The element that is often lost: The key element of planning for life is service. Each of us will inevitably serve. But what and who will we serve? And will our service make a difference?

Living for ourselves is an empty shell of a life. Such a hollow existence has little meaning: Neither to ourselves or others.

But a life of service—making a difference in the lives of others—will have great meaning. Not just to others, but also to ourselves.

But making a difference also requires planning. It requires good planning as well as execution.

To make a doable plan and then execute that plan according to the plan require effective planning tools. They also require techniques that allow us to start from where we are now to where we want to be according to a practical and appropriate timeline.

To live a life of meaning means having a purpose. And having a purpose is infective.

So not only can we create a plan to make a difference in the lives of others. That purpose and planning will automatically influence others to also make a difference in the lives of others around them.

In other words, making a difference is infective. It is like lighting a match in a withered field of grass. The grass will ignite and the fire will spread.

In this book we will examine a range of techniques and facilities that will help you develop a plan for life that makes a difference. A plan that gives meaning and purpose for our lives.

This includes helping us examine ourselves and develop an inventory of skills.

There are sections of this book that explain the science of some of these tools. Feel free to skip over these sections if the nuts and bolts of these techniques don't interest you. The main principles are easy enough to accomplish by themselves.

This book will then give us the tools to create our plan with timelines and benchmarks. We will utilize techniques to visualize, embrace and execute our plan. These together provide the means for accomplishing those goals that give our life meaning.

I would like to add that we have included several ready-to-use forms inside this book. If you would like to download these forms, simply go to the website https://www.caseadams.com/plan-for-life-forms/.

Chapter One

What is Your Plan for Life?

First let's ask and answer a question: What is personal strategic planning?

Personal strategic planning is the process of creating a personal plan for life that engages a number of specific areas of interest. Who determines these areas of interest? You do, of course!

This doesn't mean that you would choose areas of interest whimsically. These areas would be developed from your very personal goals in life.

Saying that, we're still living in the practical world. As such, there are matters of practical necessity that will likely be common among each of your strategic plans. These of course include issues of physical survival, which naturally relate to your career choices, your financial goals, health, family issues and so forth.

But as we will cover in this course, these issues of practical survival must be tied in with your deeply personal goals about your life: What do you want to accomplish with your life? When you are near the end of your life, or simply retired and looking back at your life, what will you want to have accomplished over the years?

As your goals and objectives are exercised in the form of strategic planning, we find they are interlaced. They provide an interlocked pattern that will draw us out into our future, and cohesively blend into a lifetime of activities that tie our goals together.

Let's use a simplistic example. Let's say that an athlete is competing in a track race that he wants to win. But he is also courting a girl who is attending the race alone.

She is sitting up in the bleachers. Due to his combination of goals, the track athlete will certainly stop by the girl's bleacher seat and say hello before he goes onto the track. Why? Because he is trying to accomplish two goals concurrently.

This is what we do during our lives. We naturally eye up multiple goals and try to accomplish them simultaneously, often without a plan.

But what if the girl tells the athlete that she wants to leave and wants the young man to skip the race and take her out for a milkshake? What will the young man do?

This is where priorities come in. If the young man has set up his priorities correctly, he will easily be able to navigate the situation. He will automatically know which takes the highest priority in his life.

Certainly, part of this is how these current and short term goals tie into his larger goals. How important is this track race anyway? Perhaps it is part of his gaining a scholarship for his college education. Or perhaps not. Perhaps finding a girl is more important to his long-term goals.

This crude example illustrates how important personal strategic planning is. We can insert any number of competing opportunities that will present to us through our life. Which are more important to us?

If we don't have a personal strategic plan, we will wander aimlessly from one opportunity to another. Furthermore, we will find that we may not execute many of our opportunities, because of our uncertainty of whether we want to do them.

Have you ever seen a child, cat or other pet jump from one toy to another? They are unsure of what toy they want to play with—or even if the toy they want is available at all.

Have you ever seen someone around you do this in life? Have you ever done this yourself? Most of us have at one time or another.

In his book, *"Dare to Prepare,"* Ron Shapiro discusses three reasons many of us don't make a plan: The first is thinking, 'I don't have time—I have too many things to do.' This means pushing forward to get things done without a plan—thinking that we can fudge our way through it as it happens.

The second reason is thinking, 'I've done this before so I don't need to plan.'

The third reason is thinking, 'I know how to do this.' This is over-confidence, plain and simple.

Such over-confidence leads to arrogance. And this leads to becoming sloppy, and not being able to execute.

This brings us to an essential part of any plan for life: Humility. When we approach our life with humility, we understand that life will challenge us. And because life will challenge us, we must become prepared for its challenges.

And in order to become prepared to face life's challenges, we must make a plan.

As we'll learn, our strategic plan should be written, but it will remain a living document. It will provide us with a tool for measuring our progress, as well as a tool for succeeding in accomplishing our goals.

By the end of this book, you should develop the following skills and knowledge and be able to:

- Understand how visualization and documenting strategic plan increases the likelihood of accomplishing your goals.

- Develop your personal mission statement.
- Define your personal vision.
- Produce your personal inventory, including your assets and liabilities.
- Have a grasp of your true identity.
- Develop life-long objectives to accomplish.
- Determine timelines to accomplish life-long objectives..
- Compartmentalize and prioritize objectives into relevant categories—including financial, career, health, family, education, spiritual, and/or custom categories.
- Tie together category goals into your strategic plan.
- Develop your 20-year plan for each category.
- Develop your 10-year plan for each category.
- Develop your 5-year plan for each category.
- Develop your 1-year plan for each category.
- Develop your 6-month plan for each category.
- Develop your short-term plan for each category.
- Measure and assess your goal achievements.
- Adjust your goals as necessary.

What you will find in this book is not an abbreviated or streamlined method. I believe this will short-change our future. Can we abbreviate our lives? Certainly not. We need to live them out—each and every day.

Therefore, the more detailed our plan is—the better able we will be able to live out each day in the future.

What gives me the ability to guide you through this material? I've spent the last 30 years of my career helping to guide people. I've helped businesses and people develop their personal strategic plans and achieve their business goals. I've also been helping people achieve their personal health plans as an alternative medical practitioner (naturopath).

And of course, I've also created my own personal plan for life, and have seen the wonders of how personal plans work.

Utilizing the tools and resources I am presenting, this book will help you develop, plan and then achieve your future goals in life.

Chapter Two

Your Personal Inventory

Most of us have particular passions and interests. We also each have particular tendencies, capacities, skills, strengths and weaknesses. Each of us also has a unique personality, and an individual identity.

These together make up our personal inventory. In all, our personal inventory is like a fingerprint or our DNA—it is unique to us.

Bringing these tendencies, capacities, skills, strengths, weaknesses and passions to the forefront of our consciousness is critical for developing our Plan for Life. We need to know these things if we are going to create a practical and constructive mission and set of goals.

Our tendencies and capacities may be obvious to us by now in our lives. We might have already completed training and are working in a particular field that we feel represents our tendencies and capacities quite well.

Regardless, the self-discovery process and assessment testing in Chapter Three could be very helpful. At least skim through this and check those elements you are curious about. Perhaps you are not fully utilizing your capacities at the moment in your current occupation, for example.

Or perhaps you are looking at the possibility of a career change or a second career, and you want to know what other skills or tendencies you might have. This chapter would be very helpful for you in that case.

Finally, if you are trying to make a decision on which direction to go with your life—perhaps you are entering college and trying to determine your major and degree program. This self-discovery chapter is a necessity if you find yourself in this situation.

Most of us have had times like this in our life—a 'sudden-death' time, where we had to make a decision about which direction we wanted to take with our life.

How do we do this? Some may be inclined to follow what their parents did. Others might rebel against their parents and do the opposite. Still others may follow what their peers think they ought to do. And others may follow what instructors or counselors have advised.

This program will let you approach these decisions using a practical and scientific process. This process will help you establish your strengths and weaknesses—which will then translate into your capacities and inclinations.

Then this process will help you find your passions.

The process is developing a personal inventory.

With this personal discovery, you will be better armed with clarity on your capacities, inclinations and passions.

Self Assessment

Assessment is based upon understanding. One cannot assess something without having some understanding of it. The self-discovery process is a process of assessment. This means making a personal assessment of yourself. Such an assessment must include our core identity as well as our personality issues and inclinations. This includes assessing a combination of things:

- What my identity is
- What my strengths are
- What my weaknesses are
- What my inclinations are

- What my capacities are
- What my passions are

Taking a personal inventory means reviewing your assets and liabilities, which lead directly to developing your mission and vision statements. This is because your mission and vision statements will effectively incorporate your assets and liabilities.

What are assets and liabilities? This is an accounting of those aspects listed on the prior page, which together make up an assessment of your situation. This means what you have going for you and what challenges you have to overcome in your path towards achieving your goals.

In business strategic planning, this is often called a SWOT analysis. The SWOT analysis is used to identify:

- Strengths
- Weaknesses
- Opportunities
- Threats

While we will incorporate these concepts here, the idea of threats is more of a competitive business environment issue. Here, we will identify these as challenges. So we might call it a SWOC analysis:

- Strengths
- Weaknesses
- Opportunities
- Challenges

Acronyms aside, let's dig into taking our personal inventory.

Your Personal Balance Sheet

Take a look at the Personal Balance Sheet form on the following pages. Before beginning to fill this out, you might want to consider reading the next chapter *("Discover Yourself")*, and taking some of the self-assessments listed at the end of that chapter.

Use the form to list issues you feel about yourself for each category. You don't have to fill in each blank. And you can add notes outside of the areas labeled here. I have added some blank lines below the categories area for that.

First the assets. These are your strengths and your opportunities. They can range from the financial—such as having some savings built up to start a business—to the spiritual—to the intellectual. For example, you may list having a strong memory or the ability to solve problems quickly. They can also include physical qualities, such as having great health. Or abilities like being able to speak well in front of an audience.

In terms of opportunities, these can include having a unique potential because of our situation or expertise. This could include a degree, a skill or being in a particular group or business, or social situation.

Once you have listed these positive aspects, fill in the next section, which are areas that you feel you need to improve upon. You can use each section to remind you of areas for improvement or you can list things that are outside these areas if you wish. You don't need to enter a liability for each blank, and you can have more liabilities or assets than the blanks provide.

Notice that personal liabilities are weaknesses and challenges. Challenges simply mean things that require additional work to overcome. There are some instances where challenges might mean certain things are out of reach—but there are usually workarounds that allow us to achieve our objectives despite these.

At the same time, realism is required. Realism starts with liberally recognizing both our strengths and weaknesses. It means listing anything that comes to mind—regardless of whether we think it ties to our mission and vision.

This is not a five minute task. Take a few days to complete this. Leave the form in a place where you can add things as you think of them. You can also fill it in on the computer, allowing you to save it as you add things.

For every asset, you should have a corresponding liability or passion. Why?

First, we are speaking of a balance sheet here. In an accounting balance sheet, assets must equal liabilities and stockholders equity (sometimes called capital) on a balance sheet.

The total of the stockholder's equity is added to the liabilities, and this must equal the total of the assets.

Why, some ask, would the stockholder's capital be added to the liabilities? Why wouldn't the stockholder's equity be an asset to the company?

Because the stockholder's equity is basically owed to the stockholders. The stockholders have invested in the company. This means if the company were ever disbanded, the stockholders would deserve their investment back after all the assets were sold and the liabilities were paid off.

Your Life Plan
Personal Inventory Worksheet

Name: _____

Date: _____

Assets	Strengths and Skills	(Optional) Weight
Body		
Mind		
Spirit		
Career		
Social		
Total Assets		

Liabilities	Areas Requiring Improvement	(Optional) Weight
Body		
Mind		
Spirit		

YOUR PERSONAL INVENTORY

Personal Inventory Worksheet

Name: _____

Date: _____

_____

Career

_____

_____

Social

_____

Total Liabilities

Passions	Areas Passionate About	(Optional) Weight
Body		
Mind		
Spirit		
Career		
Social		

Total Passions

Liabilities Plus Passions

The Role of Passions

First understand that we are not speaking of "passion" as some might desire some material object. We're not talking about materialism or sex, money, or fame here. We are discussing a passion for accomplishing something. A passion for helping others somehow. A passion for achieving something purposeful in our lives.

On our personal balance sheet, we are replacing what would be the stockholder's equity or capital area with passions. This is because our passions serve to balance out the difference between our strengths and weaknesses.

How do we know what we are passionate about?

Something we are passionate about shouldn't be too hard to determine. Something that we're passionate about should actually burst out of us.

To illustrate this: We might be at a social gathering and bored by the basic "how's the weather" discussions. But suddenly, someone says something that interests us and we find ourselves completely engaged in the conversation. We have strong opinions about it and we find ourselves putting forth those opinions.

This is a passion. We became engaged about the topic because we passionate about that topic. That's why we were suddenly engaged in the conversation.

Here are a few passions one might have:

- Turning around poverty in some part of the world
- Gaining knowledge in a particular area
- Stopping some type of crime
- Sailing around the world
- Finding a cure for a particular disease

These are only a few examples. But notice that most are quite specific. This is important. The more specific our passion is the better.

Of course, some passions are more altruistic than others. And those with moral conviction are likely to endure. But this doesn't mean we are limited when listing our passions here.

So why are passions added to our personal liabilities? Because our passions will require us to draw down our assets—now or at some time in the future.

Let's use an example. Let's say that in our assets section, we list that we have a good savings account. Yes, this may seem like a mundane example of an asset, but surely it is because such an asset can also be used for achieving education or any number of things.

But for the sake of this example, let's say that we have a savings account in our assets list, but then we also have a passion, "sailing around the world" in our Passions category.

Do you think that we can sail around the world for free? Nope. A sailboat will draw down our savings account, as we will be outfitting the boat for the trip and finding the time to make the long sail around the world.

Then we'll be drawing upon our sailing skills.

This should go for any of our passions. Our passions are those things we specifically want to use our assets for.

Using another example, say an asset that one has on the personal balance sheet is a college education. And one of this person's passion is stopping crime. Such a person would likely have to use their college education to complete a law degree so they could get into a position of affecting the system in such a way to reduce crime.

Remember that things you are passionate about should not be your specific mission statement or what will be your goals. They are specific areas you are passionate about—which should ultimately be drivers for your mission and your objectives.

Yet they don't have to be. For example, you might list a passions like "Baseball" or "Philosophy." These may be approached more like hobbies or recreation, and may not be included in our mission or primary objectives in life. But they well may appear in a secondary manner as we consider matters of wellness (in the case of baseball) or intellectual matters such as philosophy.

So how do we make our personal balance sheet balance?

There are two basic ways. One is to do it by count. For every single entry we make in the asset section, there should be a single entry in either the liabilities section or the passions section. For example, if we have 20 asset entries, and we have 15 liability entries, we should have 5 passions entered. Then the liability plus passions will equal the 20 asset entries.

The other way to do this would be to rank—or weight—each of the entries, according to importance. For example, an asset of "Good discipline" might get a weight of 5, while an asset of "Savings account" might only get a weight of 1. Why? Because money can be easily exhausted while discipline can help us reach our ultimate goals in the long run. It's sort of a rock-paper-scissors comparison.

If we choose this method, we can now add up the weighted rankings of each entry, and make sure that we have a balance between assets and liabilities plus passions.

You can use either method, or you can just assume they will balance out in the end. If you have several listings in each category, you are probably fine.

But if you see a great imbalance between the three categories, you are not thinking in balance about yourself. If there are a lot more assets than liabilities plus passions, then you might be too confident about yourself. Perhaps you aren't seeing areas that need improvement as you should.

And if there are a lot more liabilities than assets, then perhaps you aren't giving yourself enough credit for the things that you are good at. Or perhaps your passions are overwhelming your abilities to accomplish them.

So make sure that you create a credible balance between your personal assets, personal liabilities plus passions.

Now if you want to get into more detail to check your balances, you can grade the importance of an asset or liability. You can do this by putting a number alongside the column to the right.

These numbers would be according to their importance to you. Areas that you believe are particularly important or areas that you are particularly concerned about get the highest score. Those areas that seem more minute or minor would get the lowest scores.

If you do it this way, then the total of your assets should balance out to the total of your liabilities. If they don't balance, then you need to either add something on one side or another, or change the score on something to get it right.

Now this may seem arbitrary, but I guarantee you, it isn't. Once you list all of these things, your real life will begin to percolate the results, and you'll find yourself—even years later—making changes to your inventory that may increase your assets and reduce your liabilities.

This will, of course, allow you to expand upon your passions.

But if you and when you come back to this inventory process—which I would suggest at least every five years—then you should also find new liabilities about yourself. This means finding new areas that you would like to improve about yourself. New ways to grow, in other words.

Before you finalize your inventory and balance sheet, I would suggest you read through the next chapter and take at least a couple of assessments listed at the end.

Chapter Three

Discover Yourself

In this inventory phase of our Plan for Life, we are encouraged to delve deeper to understand ourselves.

As we examine our objectives in life, it is critical that we ask the most basic question: Who am I?

This of course follows one of the most famous axioms—ascribed to Greek philosophers including Socrates and Pythagoras—is to "know thyself."

This axiom was also inscribed on the entrance to the internal temple of ancient Egyptian Luxor. It was also inscribed at the entrance of the Temple of Apollo at Delphi. Similar sayings have been prevalent among other ancient societies.

Why was this question so important? Because happiness and achievement are specifically tied to this question. This translates to the necessity of understanding ourselves before we can thoughtfully and thoroughly develop our Plan for Life.

Our exploration can start with the obvious physical attributes:

- Name:
- Age:
- Gender:
- Ethnicity:
- Occupation:
- Blood type:
- Emotional type:
- Occupation:

But is that all? We have to look a bit deeper.

Before we can fully understand the nature of our physical existence, we must understand its driving force. What is the source of the energy and life of the body? Who or what is running the body? What makes up our personality?

This also relates to the issue of life itself: Is each of us simply a temporary physical body? Are we simply cellular machines that decompose after a few decades?

If we ask someone their identity, they will most likely describe their body's physical features. Or perhaps their body's country of origin. They might say "I am American" or "I am black" or "I am five feet tall, weigh 125 lbs, and female with brown eyes."

If so, what happens if our body gains 100 lbs of weight? Or we lose an appendage or get a facelift? Does my identity change?

Most of us believe our identity runs deeper than our physical body. A person with a black body wants equality with a person with a white body because that person considers that beneath the skin, we all have equality. Similarly, an obese person wants to be treated equally with someone of a more slender stature. Why would we request equality unless we are assuming we have deeper identities?

Most of us perceive the age of our body as a central part of our identity. If we have an older body, we identify ourselves as an older person. If we have a younger body, we think of ourselves as a child or teenager.

Yet these change with time. The child body becomes an older body within a few decades. And with time comes a new type of body. Yet we are still the same person, right? The same person who was a child is now older. It is not that there is a change of identity over the years.

Rather, simply the body has aged, just as a car might age or a house might age.

As a result of this problem, most of us try to deny the age of our body in one respect or another. Teenagers want to be older and more mature and older adults want to be younger and more youthful.

Indeed, most adults refuse to accept getting old. As any birthday party will illustrate, adults try to disconnect ourselves from the physical age of our body somehow.

As a result, older people will hide their age. We become embarrassed by our body's age as we get older. For this reason, many older adults do not want to state their age. They want to distance themselves from the age of their body. Why?

Because we do not think we are old. We feel different from the age of our body because we are different from that body.

As science has debated this topic, there have been two general views: The first assumes a machine-like information-processing generating system with various modules of activity, all competing for control. This "chaos-machine" theoretically builds upon a system of learning and evolution without any central person or actor.

The other, more prevalent view historically, portrays the body as driven by an inner self or life force, central and governing to the body's existence.

Among proponents of this inner self model, there is also some debate regarding the characteristics of the inner self. Some suggest it is a small part of the living organism. They refer to the "soul" as a type of "moral organ."

Others refer to the soul as part of some kind of trinity: *"body, mind and spirit."* Still others consider the inner self as the central component of life. Debate on this topic continues, but empirical information and clear research data clarifies the conclusion.

What Body Part are You?

Following an arm amputation due to an infection or other injury, no one would claim the amputee is any less of a person. This is because the same personality is there despite the massive structural change in body.

This logic can be extended to even severe cases such as the loss of both arms and legs or other major parts of the anatomy. An explosion or other traumatic accident might leave ones torso intact while amputating both the body's arms and legs.

Regardless of losing these appendages, the person is still perceived as a whole person—the same person as before—even though their body cannot function the way it did before. The person who operates the body still contains the same conscious being with the same personality.

This is why paraplegic and quadriplegic rights are protected by law, and why quadriplegic Steven Hawking is considered one of the today's foremost theoretical physicists despite physical handicaps. Physically disabled people are given equal rights because society considers these persons equal in all respects, despite any deficiencies in their physical bodies.

The physical organs can illustrate the same logic. It is now commonplace in medicine to surgically remove and replace organs such as kidneys, livers, hearts, hips and other parts in order to preserve the healthy functioning of the body. Some parts—like hearts and hip sockets—are now replaced with artificial versions.

Modern medicine has illustrated through many years of organ transplants that a person's identity does not travel with the organ. Otherwise, we might have—as a few comedic theatrical performances have suggested—people whose personalities reflect their organ donors. Imagine someone receiving a heart transplant and assuming part of the personality of the dead donor.

We might compare this to an auto accident: Let's say a car is brought into a repair shop after a collision: The shop determines the car needs the tires changed, the engine rebuilt and various other parts of the car replaced before the car can be put back on the road.

These changes and new car parts do not affect the driver of the car. The driver will still be the same person no matter how many new parts are put on the car. After the engine is rebuilt, the new tires installed and the other parts replaced, the unchanged driver gets back into the car and drives it away.

The Lifeless Body

By any physical observation made in the death of any living being, life leaves the body during death. When we see a living body full of life, movement, energy, personality, and purpose, we understand these symptoms of life are residing within the body.

When death arrives, suddenly those symptoms of life leave: There is no movement, no energy, and no personality remaining within the dead body. The body becomes lifeless. There is no growth, no will, no personality and no purposeful activity.

For thousands of years, doctors and scientists have autopsied, dissected and otherwise examined millions of dead bodies. No one—not even modern researchers with technical medical instruments—has been able to find any chemical or physical element missing from the dead body that was present when the body was alive.

The dead body has every physical and material component the living body had. All of the cells are still there. The entire DNA is still there. All of the nerves, the organs, the brain and central nervous system—every physical element—is still resident in the cadaver.

The life force of the body has never been seen under a microscope or by any other physical piece of equipment. Furthermore, since this living force separates from the body at death, leaving an intact physical body with no life, it is obvious that this life force is not part of the body.

Since the personality is also gone when this life is gone from the body, it would also be logical that our personality is part of this life force, and not part of the physical body—again since the physical body including all the DNA and neurons remains.

Just as the driver is not the car, he or she may be driving. The driver can step out of the car at any time. Therefore, the driver logically has a separate identity from the car.

This concept pervaded during the time of the Greek philosophers. Plato, Aristotle, Ptolemy, Socrates, Hippocrates, Pythagoras and others all ascribed to this notion. Hippocrates professed that the life within the body was due to a "vital spirit" within, which acted through four different humors, for example.

When one of Socrates' students asked him how he wanted to be buried, Socrates gave them a clear reply:

They could do whatever they wanted with the body, because he would be long gone by then.

Are You the Cells?

Throughout its physical lifetime, our body is continually changing, yet we continue to maintain our core identity and consciousness. Research has shown all living cells in the body have a finite lifespan, ranging from minutes to days to years.

It is thought a few cells of the body—such as certain bone marrow stem cells and brain cells—may exist through the duration of the body. Still there are only a handful of these cells compared to the estimated 200 trillion cells making up the body.

By far the vast majority of cells in the body will participate in cell division. Following division, older cells time out and are broken down by the immune system and discarded, leaving the newly divided cells in their place.

Using this process the body constantly sloughs off older cells from the body, replacing them with new ones. Different cells in different parts of the body have different death clocks. For example:

- Intestinal cells are replaced between two and five days
- Stomach lining cells are replaced between two and ten days
- Neutrophil and eosinophil blood cells are replaced within five days
- Lung alveoli cells are replaced within eight days
- Blood platelets are replaced within 10 days

- Epidermis skin cells are replaced within a month
- Osteoblast bone cells are replaced within 90 days
- All liver cells are replaced within 18 months
- Most stem cells are replaced within 3-5 years
- All fat cells are replaced within 8 years
- All bone cells are replaced within 10 years
- All heart cells are replaced within 10 years
- All bone cells are replaced within 10 years

Nerve cells and retinal cells can live for decades, and some over the lifetime of the body. In 2005, research from the Lawrence Livermore National Laboratory and Sweden's Karolinska Institute utilized carbon-14 analyses to examine cell lifetime in the brain.

They discovered that many of the brain's cells are generated when the body is young, and many brain and nervous system cells will be replaced over the body's lifetime.

They found that these longest-living cells will still recycle much of their atomic composition: The exception is some of the nucleotides within the brain cells' genetic matter, which turnover more slowly.

However, the composition of all cells will turn over. Every cell is made up of ionic and molecular combinations. The atoms that make up these molecular combinations are constantly being replaced. Our cells' cytoplasm, organelles and membrane will thus be composed up of recycled atoms.

This is all supported by the science. Research in the 1950s led by Dr. Paul Aebersold at the Oak Ridge Atomic

Research Center concluded that approximately 98 percent of the atoms composing the body are replaced every year.

Furthermore, as we'll discuss later in the book, our body contains more bacteria than cells.

Microbiologists have estimated that the typical human organism contains ten times more bacteria than cells. The typical body may contain about 200 trillion cells. But our body will also contain about 2,000 trillion bacteria units, of hundreds of different species.

Each of these bacteria are single-celled living creatures. Yes, like our cells, bacteria have cell walls and cytoplasm and organelles. They also typically have a short lifespan.

Our body's bacteria will reproduce by division anywhere from a few minutes to a few hours. So like most of our cells, the precise makeup of our bacteria is also constantly undergoing change as well.

However, unlike our cells, bacteria are also living organisms in themselves.

As we'll discuss later, bacteria have consciousness. They will communicate with each other using quorum sensing along with biochemical secretion. Indeed, bacteria also communicate with their host (our bodies) utilizing cytokines and other biochemicals. In this way, they can stimulate the body's immune system and also help regulate the body's moods and biorhythms.

Our body cannot survive without these bacteria. They are critical to the body's health. But these bacteria are not us. They are independent living entities.

Understanding our bacteria are separate from us; our physical bodies change nearly every cell within days, weeks or years; and every atom and molecule is replaced from the food we eat, the water we drink and the air we breathe; *the body we were wearing five years ago is not the same body we are wearing today.* We are wearing a completely recycled body. In effect, we have each *changed bodies.* Every rhythmic element of matter—every vibrating atom—has changed.

This might well be compared to a waterfall. The water within a waterfall is always changing. From moment to moment, the waterfall will be made up of different water. Therefore, the waterfall we see today is not the same waterfall we saw yesterday.

Since each of us is the same person from moment to moment and year to year within an ever-changing body, logically we each have an identity separate from this temporary vehicle. We cannot be the body, since the body has been replaced while we are still here. Should we look at our photograph taken five years ago, we will be looking at *a completely different body* from the one we are wearing today. The eyes looking at the eyes in the picture will be different eyes.

Our body is a fluid structure. It is a complex recycling mechanism that supports life. Not only does it support trillions of microorganisms. This mechanism supports a living entity within—a living being separate from the body's ever-changing cells, molecules, atoms and bacteria.

What about the DNA in the cells?

More recently it has been proposed that our core identity is our DNA.

This hypothesis is based upon the genetic matter being located not only among every cell, but with the brain cells.

Because brain cells live longer, the DNA may be retained through the life of the body.

This said, the vast majority of the atoms that make up our DNA throughout our body are replaced within a few years.

This assumption leap revolves around a proposal that the chemical combinations that make up our DNA somehow have developed the desire to survive. As if our DNA seeks to survive.

Have we ever observed chemical combinations wanting to survive? Chemicals or their combinations do not display this characteristic. Outside of a living organism, chemicals do not seek survival. Chemicals may react and form various substances, and certainly will change structure when heated or cooled.

The desire to survive is connected to the desire to improve survival factors and eliminate threats to survival. The need to improve survival requires someone who values survival over death.

In fact, many chemicals actually work to shorten the survival of the body. They act like toxins within the body. They do not seek survival in themselves.

Chemicals that value their own existence means that the chemicals could somehow recognize a difference between living chemicals and dead chemicals. This in turn requires that chemicals have awareness, because the desire to survive requires an awareness of self-existence. It also requires a fear of death: Could a chemical become afraid to die?

To be able to desire survival, a living organism must be aware that it is alive. This means differentiating between itself and a batch of dead chemicals.

If there is no distinction between life and death, survival is a moot point. Why desire survival if non-living chemicals are being avoided?

Chemicals have a different mechanism. Chemicals follow the laws of physics related to motion and movement. This includes the first law of thermodynamics: The total energy of a system remains constant. It can be transformed from one state to another, but unless that energy is transformed, there is no change in energy. This is also communicated as the law of energy conservation.

This means that a chemical cannot suddenly obtain from within itself the desire (an energy) to survive. Chemicals are lifeless unless they are energized by an outside life force.

A small unicellular organism can become subject to many environmental challenges. These include freezing, direct sun exposure and any number of natural enemies. If there were no distinction between living or dead chemicals, the path of least resistance would be to remain dead chemicals.

Why try to survive without a benefit for living? If there were no awareness and desire for survival in the face of all this resistance, there would be no incentive for genes to develop and evolve towards greater complexity—the basic tenet of the evolutionary theory and the 'survival of the fittest.'

Put more simply, if a living entity could not distinguish itself from a nonliving entity, there would be no urge to survive. Without the urge to survive, there would be no motivating factor to encourage adaptation or mutation. There would be no impetus to evolve because survival is not valuable without an awareness of life.

DNA is composed of unique combinations of nucleotides. The bases for these nucleotides are either cytosine (C), guanine (G), adenine (A) or thymine (T)

Where is the self located within these chemicals? Is it one of these? Or is the self resident in the combination?

If so, can we extract a DNA combination and it will spawn new ones and come together to form a body? Or will the individual DNA seek survival in any sense?

No. Extracted DNA becomes lifeless once it is removed from a living organism.

The selfish gene hypothesis has no logical basis. It also has no experimental support. And no observational support. Genes cannot desire survival. They cannot mutate, or make changes that promote survival without an underlying conscious self present within the organism—a self who values life and wants to survive.

This living self must be aware that it is alive, and must therefore value survival. Once the self values survival, it has a logical basis for driving genetic and physiological adjustments to better adapt to the environment. Because the self is fundamentally alive when it is inserted into a temporary physical body, it naturally strives to survive within that organism.

Personality arises from Consciousness

The proposal that personality is determined by genetic code is refuted by children who have inherited genes from parents. Children are each born with distinct personalities, talents and character traits not necessarily portrayed in their parents or grandparents. While we are quick to notice similar physical traits among our children, each has their own character and personality.

We can easily observe children behaving significantly different from their parents in similar situations. We can also witness the many conflicts that arise between children and parents. We have also observed that the extraordinary talents of child music geniuses or savants are not passed down genetically. In most musical savant cases, the parents have relatively little or no musical gift whatsoever.

If personality and behavior were genetically driven then genetically identical twins would live parallel lives and have identical personalities. They would make the same decisions, leading to identical histories.

This is not supported by the research. Twins live dramatically unique and individual lives from each other. Depending upon how much time they spend together, they will make distinctly different choices in life as well. In general, they display significantly unique and often diverse behavior.

In 2007, Hur and Rushton studied 514 pairs of two to nine year old South Korean monozygotic (identical) and dizygotic (non-identical) twins. Their results indicated that only 55% of the children's pro-social behavior related to genetic factors and 45% was attributed to non-shared environmental behavior. It should also be noted that shared environmental factors could not be eliminated from the 55%, so the genetic influence was likely must less than even the 55%.

In another study from Quebec, Canada, an analysis of 292 mothers demonstrated that maternal behavior only accounted for a 29% genetic influence at 18 months and 25% at 30 months. In a study of 200 African-American twins, including 97 identical pairs, genetics accounted for about 60% of the variance in smoking.

In a study done at the Virginia Commonwealth University's Institute for Psychiatric and Behavioral Genetics, a large sampling revealed that individual behavior was only about 38-40% attributable to genetics, while shared environment was 18-23% attributable and unshared environmental influences were attributable in 39-42%. These studies are also confirmed by others, illustrating a large enough variance from 100% to indicate the presence of an individual personality within each twin.

Distinct identity despite genetic sameness is further evidenced by the fact that identical twins will have distinctly different fingerprints, irises and other physical traits, despite their identical genetics. Many twins also differ in handedness and specific talents. Researchers have found that twins will often have significantly different lifestyle choices later in life such as sexual preference, drug abuse, and alcoholism.

For example, say two people purchase the exact same make, model and year automobile at the same time. Comparing the two cars in the future will reveal the cars had vastly different engine lives and mileages. They each had different types of breakdowns, and different problems.

This is because each car was driven differently. One was likely driven harder than the other was. One was likely better taken care of than the other was. They may have been the same make and model, but each had different owners with different driving habits.

Because twins have the same genetics—just as the cars shared the same make and model—the unique factors related to the eventual circumstances of their lives stem from the fact that each body contains a distinct driver.

What about the Brain and Mind?

One might propose that since we have yet to transplant someone's brain maybe we are the brain. Most of us have heard of the famous neurosurgical experiments first documented by Dr. Wilder Penfield, where he stimulated the temporal cortex and stimulated particular memories in subject during brain surgery. These results and their confirmations left scientists with an impression that life must reside in the brain since emotional memories were stimulated with the electrode testing.

This assumption is disputed by other brain research over the past fifty years on both humans and animals, however. The assumption that the emotional self is contained in the brain has been conflicted by the many cases of intake emotions and memory following the removal of brain parts and even a majority of the brain.

In 1978, Mishkin documented that the removal of either the amygdala or the hippocampus did not severely impair memory. Mumby later determined that memory was only mildly affected in rats with hippocampus and amygdala lesions.

According to a substantial review done by Vargha-Khadem and Polkey in 1992, numerous hemidecortication surgeries—the removal of half the brain—had been conducted for a number of disorders.

In a majority of these cases, cognition and brain function continued uninterrupted. A few cases even documented an improvement in cognition. Additionally, in numerous cases of intractable seizures, where substantial parts of brain have been damaged, substantial cognitive recovery resulted in 80 to 90% of the cases.

These and numerous other studies illustrate this effect—called *neuroplasticity*. In other words, the inner self is not reduced by brain damage or removal. The same person remains after brain parts are removed. The same personality remains. There may be reduced brain function, or those functions may be moved to other brain locations.

The majority of stroke patients go about living normal lives afterward as well. Even in cases where memory, cognitive and/or motor skills are affected by cerebrovascular stroke, the person within is still present, and though handicapped, remains unaffected by the physical changes in the brain.

Memory, sensory perception and the emotional self-concept are not brain-dependent. Many organisms have memory and sensory perception without having a brain. Bacteria, for example, do not have brains, yet they can memorize a wide variety of skills and events, including what damaged or helped them in the past.

Other organisms such as plants, nematodes and other organisms are living replete with memory and recall without having brains.

MRI and CT brain scans on patients with various brain injuries or stroke have shown that particular functions will often move from one part of the brain to another after the original area was damaged.

We must therefore ask: Who or what is it that moves these physical functions from one part of the brain to another? Is the damaged brain area making this decision? That would not make sense. Some other guiding function must be orchestrating this move of the function. Who or what is guiding this process?

The retention of memory, emotion, and the moving of brain function from one part of the brain to another is more evidence of a deeper mechanism; an *operator* or *driver* within the body who is *utilizing* the brain—rather than *being* the brain. The driver is the continuing element. Physical structures continually undergo change, while the driver remains, adapting to those changes.

Biofeedback

In biofeedback, sensors are attached to various parts of the body to monitor physical responses like heart rate, breathing, brainwaves, skin response, muscle activity, and so on. These sensors are connected to a computer, which displays the various response levels onto a monitor for the subject to see. The heart rate amplitude and frequency readings will be displayed on the monitor in waves, bars, and/or numbers.

With a little practice, most people—once they see their heart rate with graphics clearly on the monitor—can consciously lower their heart rate with intention. Biofeedback has thus been used successfully to teach people to alter physical functions such as muscle tension, hunger, physical stress, and other autonomic functions.

Biofeedback training gives the subject the ability to directly control a variety of physical responses including stomach cramps, muscle spasms, headaches, and other occurrences—many known to be part of a biochemical cascade.

The reason why the biofeedback subject can learn to control certain biochemical messenger driven autonomic functions is that the self ultimately exists outside the biochemistry of the body. The self is the key participant who influences physical functions. Once the person intends to make a change, the mind will facilitate the stimulation of the biochemicals by the appropriate glands to produce a physiological response.

Sometimes this can take time, discipline or practice. Even without biofeedback, a person can initiate various autonomic responses. Most of us have experienced how a physiological fear response may be initiated by simply imagining a dangerous event or situation. This happens every day in the professional world, where executives stress over events that have not happened nor may never happen.

This stress increases the heart rate and stimulates stress-biochemical release. Most of us have experienced being worried about an event that may never happen. The resulting increase in our heart rate indicates our body's autonomic response to an over-anxious self.

If the self can affect the body's biochemistry with anxiousness, the self is separate from the biochemistry. Furthermore, if the self can affect the body's biochemistry intentionally, there is no question of the self's ability to direct the body through intention. The range of control the self has over the body is limited by design. Still, there is no doubt that intention initiates the sequencing of instructional messaging through the body.

This neurochemical process would be analogous to a computer operator operating a computer. A computer will tabulate, calculate, and memorize data. It will display various graphics and perform various functions, based upon the input or direction of the operator. The software and hardware are designed in such a way to coordinate computer functions very quickly and automatically within particular limitations.

Regardless of the programming, the operator is required. The computer operator must decide to turn on the computer and must decide to input into the machine certain intentional commands to initiate the computer's programming functions. In the same way, the physical body, with all of its functional chemistry and various physical responses, is ultimately being steered by the personality within: this is the self, the living being—the operator of the body.

It is difficult sometimes to separate the self inside the body from the various physical and biochemical operations of the body. This is because the feedback-response system bridges the self with the physical body.

For example, breastfeeding is now being rediscovered. Researchers have discovered breast-feeding not only gives the child better nourishment and a stronger immune system, but also renders a better temperament and brain development due to some of the biochemistry of breast milk. This notion is consistent with the observation of various nutrients or drugs altering moods and behavior.

Chemicals influence behavior because they not only stimulate physical tissue response, but they also give feedback to the self about what is going on in the body. For example, the feeling of thirst is a neurochemical signal to the self that the body needs water. The combination of hormonal, osmotic, ionic and nerve signaling all integrate to stimulate osmoreceptors located among brain tissue (such as the anteroventral third ventricle wall).

Once stimulated, these receptors initiate waveform signaling through the hypothalamus, which converts into the more subtle waveforms of the mind. Through the reciprocation of the mind, the self observes this feedback, and responds by initiating action to find some water.

A computer will also feed back to its operator in the same way. The computer is not only designed to perform operations based upon the input of the operator, but also its programming is designed to feed back to the operator the results of those operations, signaling a need for new responses from the operator.

This process is called a feedback loop. The body's feedback system is designed to respond to environmental and physical changes around the anatomy. The system is designed to signal to the self on how the body is functioning. This is one of the purposes for serotonin release in the body: To feed back the presence of balance within particular organs and tissue systems.

A diet balanced in proteins, carbohydrates, and fats, along with physiological activities stimulate the conversation of tryptophan to serotonin. This conversion is also stimulated by such activities as relaxation, laughter, and exercise.

These are all positive activities for the body's metabolism. This combined state of balance and activity results in a normal flow of serotonin, which feeds back through the brain's translation systems to the self the presence of physiological balance among certain parts of the body.

Pain, on the other hand, indicates quite the opposite: Some imbalance exists somewhere. Pain feeds back to the operator the need for an adjustment among certain functions or activities. This necessary adjustment could be to the diet, fluid intake, sitting posture, lack of exercise, or perhaps an infection of some sort. Chronic pain indicates an unresolved lack of balance in the body, requiring an appropriate response to fix the issue.

Just as an instrument panel on an automobile informs the driver of the running condition of car, we can monitor the condition of our body through these and other neurochemical feedback mechanisms.

Just as the car driver slows down when the speedometer shows the car is over the speed limit, the self—directly through conscious control or indirectly through the autonomic system—can make the needed adjustment when the body's feedback systems indicates a problem.

The Personality Within

The evidence indicates the existence of a transcendental inner self operating the body. This is the true "I" of our existence. The self is the source of personality and life, which the body expresses through physical activity over its lifetime.

Since there is energy, personality and movement in a living body prior to death, followed by a lack of movement, personality and energy afterward, the source of the energy and personality must leave the body at death. Contrary to the proposals of many, since each personality is unique and different from all other personalities, each self must be an independent, individual being.

Many philosophers have proposed that after death, the living being either fades into "nothingness," or expands into "everything." This philosophy proposes that the living being does not have an individual identity after death: Instead, the now individual self simply vanishes and evaporates into space.

This is often described as merging into "nothingness"—also called the void—or merging into "everything"—sometimes referred to as the white light. Still others contend that after death we merge into a vast ocean of consciousness. These two assumptions are the same proposition, because in either case the individual self loses individuality.

Rather, each individual self is a unique and distinct personality. This individuality is expressed by the special talents unique to each of us. These special talents also point to an individual existence prior to birth, as confirmed also by Dr. Stevenson's and others' work. If the self existed as an individual prior to birth and throughout a lifetime of an ever changing body, is it logical that the self would lose that individuality after death?

The inner self is the underlying source of our personality; our feelings, emotions, desires, the ability to love, and the desire to be loved. This personality is distinct from the mental programming taking place through the brainwaves and neural network of the physical body.

Beyond the physical programming, each of us retains an independent, active inner self with a central objective of happiness, and receiving and giving love. Does it appear logical that this active being—continually seeking happiness and loving relationships—would suddenly abandon these propensities and permanently merge into a state of nothingness or mass consciousness?

What should the purpose of a temporary separate existence be then? Could a collective vague consciousness or nothingness separate into a multitude of individual purpose and will? Furthermore, the living self has maintained a consistent existence throughout many decades of a changing physical body.

This equates to surviving a body that is continually dying. Does it seem logical that the fatal death of the same body would then remove our inherent will to survive and prosper? Should the death of this temporary body abruptly end our desire to love and exchange love?

Purpose and activity are the key distinctions between living and dead matter. Both of these elements (purpose and activity) indicate the existence of individuality. The very definition of consciousness requires individuality. Consciousness requires awareness. Awareness of something or someone requires an individual consciousness separate from that object or person being *aware* of. Thus, an 'ocean of consciousness' would logically be an oxymoron.

Consistent with the ancient teachings of all major religions, the ancient philosophers and the vast majority of western scientists prior to the emergence of the concept of an incidental accidental evolution of species, we propose the existence of a unique individual being transcendental to the gross physical plane who evolves through lifetimes of learning experiences in different physical bodies. As the inner self evolves, each progressive physical body reflects that current evolution.

Plato, Socrates and most of the ancient Greek philosophers referred to this inner self as the *soul*. The translation is thought to originate with Aristotle, who described the self with the Latin *telos*. Rather than a vague spirit-like organ, *telos* most accurately translates to a personality with purpose, will, and character. In this context, we would emphasize that each of us does not possess a soul: each of us *is* a soul, accessing the physical plane through a temporary physical body.

A baseline definition of sanity is being realistic about our identity. To live a sane, rational life requires a clear understanding of this element of our existence.

Consider, for example, a person who walks around thinking he is Abraham Lincoln, or perhaps the Pope. We might consider such a person insane, because they are identifying themselves as someone they are not.

In the same way, in order to considered sane we must also identify ourselves as we are. Given our discussion of the science in this chapter, to identify ourselves as our temporary physical body would put our intelligence into question.

Such a position would also inevitably result in disappointment as we execute our Plan for Life. Why? A lifespan that ignores our spiritual side will leave a hole in our life.

Using this strong foundation of knowledge, we are now more equipped to explore our individual talents, capacities and capabilities as opportunities.

Self-Assessments to Discover Your Capabilities

Continuing our self-discovery process, we might consider testing ourselves to see what kinds of strengths and weaknesses we have. This section is for those who seek direction in determining your best Plan for Life course. Others may want to pick and choose some of the testing in this section to see if we have chosen our best course. Or we may want to explore a possible second career or change of direction in our life.

It is important to understand that we are not necessarily limited by our capacities and capabilities. With enough willpower, most of us can hurdle much of what life wants to serve up to us.

At the same time, it may be prudent to be practical about our choices and direction. If we have certain capacities and skills, shouldn't we be encouraged to at least utilize those capabilities?

Let's say, for example, that we have great analytical skills. Should we not at least consider this as we consider a creative career? Or vice versa?

Certainly our passions and the rest of our inventory should be considered. But we might want to add some testing to our consideration, especially if we need more inventory items to balance out our passions.

This said, let's review a few tests that can reveal more about our capacities and capabilities.

Intelligence quotient assessment

This is also loosely called the IQ test. It is a test that is intended to determine several aspects of cognition:

- Problem solving skills
- Logical reasoning skills
- Spatial relationships skills
- Primary linguistic skills
- Basic calculation skills

The original intent of the IQ test was to determine a person's potential capacity. It was designed to test children, and many educators used it to decide the future course direction of students.

The first IQ test was developed by Dr. Francis Galton in the late 19th Century. The Binet-Simon IQ test of 1905 followed. This language-oriented test was intended to measure whether a child had a mental age that matched their physical age—aimed at six year-olds.

The IQ test has come a long way since then. Today's tests can be taken at any age and are set up to provide scores that relate to intelligence levels for that age group.

Today's tests utilize the Cattell—Horn—Carroll theory. This is a combination of theories of psycho lists Dr. Raymond Catthell, Dr. John Carroll and Dr. John Horn, developed between the 1940s and the 1990s.

This current testing focuses upon fluid and crystallized intelligence. Fluid intelligence relates to one's reasoning, problem-solving and concept formation. Crystallized intelligence relates to acquired knowledge. This means the ability to communicate and reason with respect to knowledge gained previously.

The current IQ tests may also focus on long- and short-term memory, visual and auditory processing, reading and writing skills, decision and reaction times and processing speeds.

If you are thinking of entering a career that requires significant cognitive skills, you might consider taking this test. Or if you are simply curious about your current cognitive skills compared to others.

One of the best tools for taking an IQ test today is the internet. This provides the ability to be walked through each question and be scored cumulatively.

Here are a couple of recommended IQ tests you could take if you want to know your current IQ levels:

https://www.psychologytoday.com/tests/iq/classical-iq-test

http://www.myiqtested.com/

DISC Personality Assessment

The DISC Personality test was developed by Dr. Walter Clarke, based upon some of Dr. William Marston's theories. These are focused upon four basic behavioral traits:

- Dominance
- Inducement
- Submission
- Compliance

These personality traits also provide the acronym this testing measures. These traits are based upon how we relate to our environment.

This primarily means how we relate to the people and organizations we are surrounded by. The DISC assessment aims to identify a person's tendency for 15 different personality patterns:

- Achiever
- Agent
- Appraiser
- Counselor
- Creative
- Developer
- Inspirational
- Investigator
- Objective Thinker
- Perfectionist
- Persuader
- Practitioner

- Promoter
- Result-oriented
- Specialist

Today this test is used by some employers and government agencies to test the ability of a person to match the needs of a particular occupation.

Here is a free online DISC test:
https://discpersonalitytesting.com/free-disc-test/

Myers-Briggs Type Indicator

The Myers-Briggs Type Indicator (MBTI) self-test is based upon Carl Jung's theories of psychological types. One's psychological types can include:

- Our personality type
- Our world of focus
- How we process information
- How we make decisions
- How we deal with structure

This assessment can be used to determine career choices or choices of schools and training. Here is a test you can take if you are interested:
http://www.onlinepersonalitytests.org/mbti

Jung Typology Test

Alternatively, we can take this test to assess what personality type related to the Myers-Briggs test. This will also reveal similar results. Here is a free online test:
http://www.humanmetrics.com/cgi-win/jtypes2.asp

Entrepreneur Profiler

Running a small business typically requires special skills. These include leadership and risk-taking. The Small Business Entrepreneur Profiler assessment measures your aptitude for launching and then running a small business.

The Entrepreneur Profiler assessment tells you if you have good aptitude for running a small business. It also suggests the kinds of businesses will likely be suitable to you. Here is an online free basic report. You can pay $5.00 for the premium version as well:

http://www.humanmetrics.com/infomate/InfoMatePass.asp

Risk Attitudes Profiler

Risk tolerance gauges our ability to handle business or workplace situations that require us to put something on the line. Having a high tolerance for risk means that we are able to put more on the line than most people.

Here is an example. Let's say that you want to start a small business, and in order to keep buying inventory and paying employees you will have to take out a small business loan.

Let's say you go to the bank and you apply for a small business loan. You supply all the information the banker needs to assess your ability to borrow the money.

The only problem is that the bank is requiring you to put up your house as collateral for the loan. This means that if your business doesn't succeed for some reason, and cannot pay the loan off, the bank can take your house.

Putting up our personal possessions for the sake of your business isn't for everyone. Some people simply couldn't tolerate that sort of risk. Many of us want to stay on the safe side.

It isn't that easy to tell how risk tolerant we might be. A good test to assess our risk tolerance is the Risk Attitudes Profiler. This online assessment is free for the basic report or it is $4.00 for a Premium Report:
http://www.humanmetrics.com/SBP/BusinessTypes.asp

Career Development Assessment

The CAD test measures our abilities to excel within a business, a workplace or team environment. Here is an online test that costs $8.95:
http://www.personalityexplorer.com/

Visionary vs. Pragramatic Test

The ability to accurately see how things will turn out in the future is a skill set described as visionary. A visionary will often excel as an entrepreneur because he or she will be able to predict how consumers will react in the future to a particular product. Or he or she will be able to understand an opportunity before it happens.

A test that measures your visionary skills or whether you are more of a pragmatist is called the Visionary vs. Pragmatist Assessment. Here is an online test that costs $3.00 to take:
http://www.humanmetrics.com/visionary/visionaryperson.asp

Back to Personal Inventory

Now that we've taken some time to do a little exploration of our identity, our skills and our capabilities, we are now ready to complete our Personal Inventory Balance Sheet.

Chapter Four

Your Mission Statement

A mission statement may sound lofty, but it is actually a practical element of planning. Saying this, we won't necessarily establish our mission statement on the first pass. It may be an evolving statement, so to speak.

A personal mission statement achieves several purposes.

A mission statement covers the "why" of our life: It answers the question: What is my purpose in life? That can be translated to "why do I exist?"

The central questions that must be answered in order to determine our life's purpose or mission relates to the practical matters of:

- Who am I? (self discovery)
- What are my strengths and weaknesses?
- What can I do with my life within my environment?
- What are my passions?
- What have others done?

The first element we discussed in Chapter Two. The rest of these elements are practical matters that will relate to our personal inventory—which we'll cover in a future discussion. This means going through a process of self-discovery, along with an understanding of what others have done that we might be able to emulate or follow in their example.

A personal mission statement will also provide us with the following:

- A focus or direction in our life
- A facility for aligning our strategies

- A basis for decision-making

However, one's mission statement should be practical. Therefore, it is best divided into practical areas. We don't necessarily have to incorporate the following, but these areas are common to most strategic plans, and therefore should be considered:

- Body: Our physical and environmental mission
- Mind: Our cognitive, emotional and intellectual missions
- Spirit: Our spiritual mission
- Career: Our professional or occupational mission
- Social: Our family, community and/or society missions

Remember again that this is just a guide to mission areas. But these five divisions divide our lives into practical areas that allow us to organize a practical strategic plan.

Let's review these divisions:

Body

The element of body relates to the physical elements. These might relate to our physical well-being and health. They may also include our relationship with our physical environment.

Mind

The element of mind includes cognitive, emotional or intellectual capacities. These can relate to our education, training and discovery. Discovery can be a key element in our mission, because learning and knowledge relate heavily to living a fulfilling life.

Spirit

The spiritual element of our mission statement can be a key fundamental for our Plan for Life—depending upon how we see ourselves and our mission in life. The importance we place upon our spiritual qualities and spiritual vision of the world provides a key aspect to what we want to accomplish in life.

Career

The career element is important to our personal strategic plan because our choice of career can affect what kind of impact we have upon the world we live in. It can also determine where we live and what kind of environment we live in. Our career mission may also tie into other elements of our Plan for Life, including our financial future, our education or training requirements, and our retirement plans.

Social

The social element of a mission statement defines how we want to relate with those around us, including family members, friends, community and society in general. What kind of social environment we want to live in, and how we might or might not want to impact those around us are also key elements. In addition, the values we place upon others and what kind of impact or influence we may have upon others during our lifetime are also important considerations.

Advantages of Compartmentalizing

By compartmentalizing our strategic plan beginning with the mission statement is an important organizational tool. It is also a tool that will help us better define and visualize our direction in life.

We may want to include other elements of our mission statement. There are no hard and fast rules. However, the element should not be too specific. It should be a generalized statement of mission—not a specific goal or accomplishment.

A good next step would be for each of us to now write out a clear mission statement for each of the specific areas. How do we write this out?

Let's use an example. Let's say, for the career category, that we want to be a lawyer. We could say we want to be a lawyer, but that would not really be a mission statement. Rather, that would be a goal. The mission statement must have purpose. For example, we might write:

"My professional mission is to become a skilled attorney in order to help those who may get into trouble."

This sort of mission extends beyond just the occupation—but defines the motives behind the choice of occupation. The mission of that occupation.

Or if one wants to become wealthy, one might say:

"My mission is to become financially well-off so that I can help others who are poor."

Again, this establishes a purpose for the accomplishment.

Why is this important? It is not just a technique, actually. It is part of the process of establishing a Plan for Life.

Let's say, for example, that one wanted to achieve a particular occupation without establishing the purpose or mission of that occupation. In the example above—just becoming an attorney in and of itself.

Such a mission statement would lead to a scenario of confusion. One might work hard in law school to achieve the accomplishment. But once they passed the bar and became an attorney, they would be left with uncertainty in terms of what kind of law they wanted to practice. They might end up floating around within the legal community and landing at a law firm doing work that left them without any sense of accomplishment.

But establishing our purpose provides us with a compass: It allows us to know more precisely why we will be working so hard to accomplish our goals. Then once we accomplish them, our mission will help direct us towards working in a way that created a greater sense of fulfillment—because of our mission.

Contributing is a critical element of our mission: Helping others in some way. If one creates a mission statement that is only self-concerning, we will be missing out on one of life's greatest rewards: Helping and loving others.

Without this aspect of our mission, we become floating islands, without a sense of relationship with the world around us. And relationship is critical to survival.

This has been confirmed over and over in research. People who become isolated from others during some part of their lives have significantly greater risks of depression and a multitude of diseases.

But those who seek to assist their fellow human in one respect or another during their lifetimes typically find accomplishment and a greater sense of fulfillment.

Measuring Missions

It is also important to have measurable missions

Remember that a mission statement must have actionable purpose. This means practical achievement is possible. And achievement means it must be measurable.

For example, in my example above about becoming a lawyer to help prevent crime, there is a measurable component here. The measurable component means the ability to test the results.

For example, such a lawyer could look back at the last year of productivity on the job and test whether his or her actions reduced crime rates in some area. Say they were a District Attorney, so they could measure the crime rates in their district.

Or the person who wants to help the poor—they should be able to measure how much they donated or provided assistance to others.

Now such a person would not necessarily be focused upon measuring their charity each year. The point is, they could if they needed to assess whether they were progressing in achieving their missions.

Summary

Let's summarize our mission statement principles:

1. Our mission statement describes the "whys" of my life. Our purpose for existing.

2. Our mission statement should be detailed enough to relate to the practical areas of our life.

3. Our mission statement should contain both the achievement and the purpose for the achievement of the mission.

4. The wording of our mission statement needs to be in actionable terms. This means utilizing the verb related to the actions we intend to take.

5. The specifics of your mission statement should be able to be measured later on, if need be.

Now its time to write your mission statements.

Exercise:

Pick a famous person that you admire. Now develop what that mission statement might have looked like for that famous person. Don't worry about whether he or she had a mission statement. Just write one up that aligns with what the famous person achieved.

Your Life Plan
Mission and Vision Statement

Name: _____

Date: _____

Vision Statement

What do I want my life to stand for?

-

_____
_____
_____
_____
_____
_____
_____
_____

Mission Statement

What is the purpose of my life?

_____
_____
_____
_____
_____
_____
_____

-

Category Mission Statements

Body

_____
_____

Mind

_____
_____

Spirit

_____
_____

Career

_____
_____

Social

_____
_____

Chapter Five

Your Vision Statement and Core Values

Before we start on our vision statement, it is useful to list a few core values in our life.

What are Core Values?

Core values are like our morals. Our life should illustrate our morals in big and small ways. Our core values include ideals that we consider important as we undertake our lives.

Our core values relate to our conscience. Things that we will never give up when we are tested. These provide the backbone for our lifestyle and our decisions as we proceed.

A useful list of considerations that might help us develop our core values:

- What are our deepest concerns?
- How important is compassion?
- How important is money?
- How important is honesty?
- How important is integrity?
- How important is discovery (learning)?

These provide a starting point to our relative core values. Remember that core values are core to us: Not our spouse, family members, profession or otherwise. We must dig deep to find these. We must own these deep inside, as they will consistently provide us with both inspiration and commitment.

Our core values will lead us to a unified vision statement.

What is a Vision Statement?

The vision statement envisions our future in a clear and concise statement. We might consider our vision to be the embodiment of our calling in life.

Calling is often misunderstood to be something related to a religious calling. Yes, a calling can be a religious calling, but it can also be a broader calling of ones life. This means a tying together of the varying purposes laid out in ones mission statement into a unifying, inspiring vision of ones life.

That is, how we see ourselves conducting our lives.

Some suggest that vision statement comes before ones mission statement. This could be so, but landing on ones vision can be difficult without having first specifying our mission and purpose in life.

A vision statement can be as short or long as we want. However, if it is too long, it will become somewhat confusing to us, and might compete with our mission statement. Our vision will be our north star or compass as we work to accomplish our life's objectives.

It is not necessary to write out ones vision statement. One can literally keep this in vision form—as a visualization. For some, this might be superior to writing it down. For others, writing down the vision statement—into a concise one or two-sentence format—is best.

Part of this depends upon whether we are a visual person or a written person. How can we tell? A visual person will not find the words that adequately describe our vision of our future. Whereas, the written person will not be able to envision something without it being in writing.

Go ahead and try it out. You will find out which one you are as you begin visualizing and/or writing it up.

Exercise:

Use the steps in this chapter to develop a vision statement and core values for a famous person you admire.

Chapter Six
Visualization Techniques

Throughout this Plan for Life system we'll be utilizing visualization in order to help us achieve our goals and objectives in life.

This chapter is intended to help you understand what visualization is and how visualization increases likelihood of accomplishing your goals. Visualization utilizes a critical tool we contain within our mind: *imagination.*

Albert Einstein said:

> *"Logic will take you from A to B. Imagination will take you everywhere."*

Visualization means using your imagination. Where can you go with your life? You can go where your imagination takes you.

Martin Eppler and Ken Platts from the University of Cambridge wrote in a 2008 paper that:

> *"Visualization can improve the quality of the strategic planning process by addressing many of its cognitive, social, and emotional challenges."*

What are some of these challenges as they apply to your Plan for Life?

Cognitive challenges

Cognitive challenges include the ability to understand how our situation can be changed in the future. We might feel we are stuck in our current environment or situation.

This might include our location, or our educational situation. Or perhaps our skills and abilities. Visualization can open up avenues to change all of these.

Visualization can wake up a plan for our way out. We may not see this way out just by thinking about the practical issues. But visualization can wake up an inner creativity that can open doors.

Cognitive challenges can also include the practical elements of developing a plan that meets with our current assets and liabilities. These can be hard to accurately assess. We will address this later on.

Social challenges

Social challenges include the pressures of family, friends and ones current socio-economic situation. This includes limitations provided by our access to education, contacts and other resources.

We can often be prisoners of the expectations of our family and friends. Perhaps our family members want us to excel in ways that contradict our values or our own vision. Or perhaps we have friends that keep us from succeeding because they are not succeeding.

These types of challenges can be almost immediately overcome with visualization.

Emotional challenges

Emotional challenges include limitations regarding our personal vulnerabilities and stresses. Past experiences can affect our emotional state.

For example, we might think that we cannot succeed in business because we have gotten cheated in the past by a slick business-person. Or perhaps we don't think that we can contribute to society because we feel that society has wronged us somehow.

Victimization

This can include what is called victimization. This is an emotional state that tends to blame others for our situation. Yes, we may have been a victim of some cruel or abusive behavior in the past. But to allow that abuse to prevent us from succeeding is to allow someone's past behavior to continue to victimize us unnecessarily.

Sometimes people do things that intentionally hurt us. Sometimes people do things to people without realizing the results of their actions, simply because they are acting in a self-centered manner.

Self-centeredness is common in this world, and it can easily block a person's vision. People can hurt others simply because their vision is blocked by self-centeredness.

This is why forgiveness is so important. If we can see our own self-centeredness, we can find a way to forgive others of their self-centeredness.

And if we can forgive others, we can put the things they did behind us. We can allow those things to fade from our consciousness over time. This will allow those things to release their grip upon us.

Confidence

Often our lack of confidence can prevent us from visualizing our own success and our ability to forge ahead with our plans for this life.

To this, many self-help consultants have gone overweight. As a result, they will stress developing an overly optimistic view of the future in order to access personal confidence.

In our Plan for Life program we stress objectivity. This means realistic assessments of what is possible, combined with our passions to allow us to create a congruent plan. This means recognizing that reaching our goals will require more than just confidence: They require a stepped organizational process, hard work, and visualization.

Yes, confidence is needed to pursue our plans. This is confidence in our abilities, and our plan. But this type of confidence is best achieved when we assess ourselves and look at our situation objectively.

In addition, we can appreciate the source of abilities comes from a Higher Power. This type of realization can help us find our confidence without unrealistically thinking we are better than we are.

In other words, what we have has been given to us by the Grace of God. We are each children of God. Our abilities and opportunities are given to us. We can embrace those or not.

Therefore, who are we to say that we are greater than this? Everything we have has been blessed upon us by a Power greater than us.

Such an outlook allows us to have confidence while maintaining a sense of humility. Without a measure of humility, how can we accept ourselves for who we are? How can we expect to achieve goals that not only raise our consciousness, but help others if we are not humble enough to make changes in our life?

Yes, confidence is good, but over-confidence can lead to over-reaching and ultimate failure to reach our goals.

Mind over Matter

To this end, there has been a great movement over the last century proposing that our thoughts influence our outcomes. While there is a solid basis for the technology, there are also limitations. In other words, the theory should not be assumed out of its context.

This *mind over matter* theory was famously proposed over a century ago by William Walker Atkinson in his book *Thought-Culture or Practical Mental Training* (1909), along with nearly a hundred other works, some under a variety of pseudonyms.

Since then, Atkinson's theories have created the framework for a multitude of self-help books over the years.

Atkinson's theories also attracted a number of followers, including influential writers such as Mary Baker Eddy of *Christian Science* fame and Wallace Wattles, author of *The Science of Getting Rich* (1910).

The governing mind philosophy of the late Mr. Atkinson and Mr. Wattles has also influenced various other works, such as *Think and Grow Rich* (1937) by Napoleon Hill, *The Greatest Salesman in the World* (1968) by Og Mandino, and the wildly popular book and movie *The Secret* (2006), by Rhonda Byrne.

These works have seduced many with unreasonable promises of material successes that emphasize wealth and fame. Many have also served to appeal to our more narcissistic natures. Why?

The error is founded upon the underlying proposals by Atkinson that we are the mind, and the mind ultimately controls the physical world. This proposition produces an unfortunate conclusion that nothing real exists except for the mind, and the mind is the creator of the universe.

This leaves us with a notion that our mind is a supreme being of sorts. This precludes the existence of a Superior Power greater than the mind. And it exaggerates our real position.

Changing the mind

The interesting part of this seductive proposal is that while the mind is theorized as the all-pervading controller of existence, the intent of these numerous self-help writings have been to help people by *changing our minds.*

The techniques proposed may vary slightly, but the intent is generally to help the reader gain greater wealth, fame, success, attention and influence by *changing* our thinking patterns and processes.

I am not arguing that the mind cannot be changed. We will utilize visualization in this text to help change our thinking. The inaccuracies I am pointing out are the hypotheses that the mind is all powerful and our identity is ultimately the mind.

The problem with this proposal is that if the person is the mind, then *who* is it that decides to change the mind? In order to change the mind there must be a driver and an observer who can intend and initiate that change of mind.

Furthermore, as noted in these works, the process required in order to change the mind is quite difficult. *Who* is the constant force making the determination to change the mind; despite all the mind's former thinking habits?

Indeed, if the mind is all-powerful, who or what could have the power to change that mind? Or is it that the mind of the self-help guru is simply greater than the mind of their student?

Lastly, *who* remains to reap the rewards once the mind has been changed? If the self is the mind, and the mind has changed, that former self is gone once the mind changes. Therefore, no one remains to realize any reward, since the last mind—the one who initially read the self-help book—is gone, replaced by the changed mind.

Which mind has the ultimate power then? The mind previous to the change or the changed mind?

Rather, the mind is a subtle sorting, translating and recording device. Yes, the mind does influence the direction of the body and its activities. But the intentional self is the driver of the mind. The mind is not the ultimate power.

The mind works with the brain much like software works with the hardware of a computer. The self drives the mind but the mind is also influenced by the senses.

The mind portrays what comes in from the senses together with the direction of the self to map its thoughts within the neural network of the brain.

One might compare this to a movie or television picture that reflects onto a movie screen or TV set. This reflection of imagery is ultimately guided by the self, but is subject to what the senses have brought in.

Let's say for example that you are a director of a movie. You have your film crew film all the scenes for the movie. Then you direct the process as the film is chopped up and edited into the final film.

As the director, you should already have an underlying aim for the movie. This is why you are called the 'director.' This direction for the movie will result in all the film being edited together.

In the same way, the person within directs the overall direction of the mind. Images from the senses will be edited together in a certain construct as directed by the self into goals and objectives.

The anatomical explanation is a little complicated. Using the images fed through the visual cortex, the brain will store and manipulate images within the posterior parietal cortex. This manipulation allows more current imagery and other sensual information to be combined with visual image history. Utilizing the posterior parietal cortex, the self can concoct and manipulate stored data in a manner consistent with its objectives and goals.

We can observe how the mind processes and manipulates sensual information when a vision or piece of music can be recalled minutes, days and even years after first being seen or heard. We can see it immediately by looking at an image, closing our eyes immediately afterward, and seeing that image imprinted onto our mind.

Our mind can also associate and compare stored data with incoming sensory images of tastes, sounds, tactile sensations and other images our senses have collected over the years. As such images are stored within the brain centers imprints these images into memory centers, the self subtly manipulates the data. This effectively directs the use of these images, cataloging them according to priority, and acting upon them subconsciously.

The mind is thus like a software program, designed to utilize the biochemical bonds within the neurons for the storage, manipulation and playback of our images and memories. This system might be compared to the recording capability of magnetic recording tape or diskettes, which store music, images, and data through magnetic arrangement.

Our manipulation of images according to our self-directed goals and objectives could be likened to the editing software for arranging and publishing videos and music.

These mental operations have a physiological basis within the brain, yet they transcend our physical actions just as the operating system software of the computer transcends the hardware operations of a computer.

Just as the software operating system provides an interfacing language between the various hardware devices of the computer, the mind uses the brain's neural networks to interact with the limbic system and brain cortices to execute commands and garner feedback regarding the condition of the body.

The mind is a changeable, subtle mechanism, yet is distinct from the person within. The separate existence of the mind can be easily shown in practical behavior: We can each observe the workings of our mind. We can watch images on the mind and see how sensory inputs become recorded and recalled.

For example, after watching a movie with special effects, we can close our eyes and watch the mental imprints of scenes of the movie within our mind.

We can also replay music recorded in the brain by the mind. We may hum or sing the words of a song we heard previously, with the tune replaying in our mind long after the song was heard. Like a television or a radio, we can also turn and change the mind's images. We can decide to change our focus from one image to another. In other words, we can direct our mind, and *change our mind*.

And this is precisely what we intend to do in Plan for Life: Change our future by changing our mind—using the techniques of visualization.

Programming the Mindscreen

Basically, visualization is the activity of using our mindscreen to picture ourselves having achieved a goal or a set of goals.

Let's use an example. Let's say you and your significant other are going on a vacation to Hawaii. What is one of the first things the two of you will do? You will each picture yourselves in Hawaii on that vacation. You will likely visualize yourselves basking on a white sand beach at the edge of a blue water ocean. Or perhaps you will visualize yourselves snorkeling together in crystal clear water.

These visualizations will accomplish a couple of things. First, they will cement your determination to complete the required tasks of purchasing tickets and reserving your hotel rooms. Second, they will provide an emotional tie to the vacation. This emotional tie will provide the convincing that the vacation will resolve your need to take a break and relax. It will also furnish a "looking-forward-to-it" stabilization.

Such a forward-looking attitude is part of our cognitive make-up. We are creatures of the forward-look. For example, we don't just open up the fridge and start eating. We will often plan our meal out. We will take the cutting board out and get some pots and pans and start preparing our meal. When we do this, we set up a forward-looking plan that includes a visualization of what the end meal might look like.

So if we can so easily visualize our meal and our vacation, why can't we visualize our future accomplishments? Why can't we use the same visualization techniques described above for our vacation to achieve goals that align with our mission in life?

We can. It simply takes a little forethought. Some creativity. Some clear techniques. And some practical realities.

Practical Realities

These are required because if we don't visualize from a practical standpoint, we'll certainly end up frustrated.

In our vacation visualization, for example, we visualized the white sand beach and the blue ocean. These are very practical. We've seen pictures of Hawaii and we know this is possible. But if we visualized going snowboarding in Hawaii, we'd likely be disappointed when we got there. Our snowboarding visualization would be impractical and unachievable. That visualization would not only be a waste of time. It would lead to frustration.

In the same way, as we visualize accomplishing goals in our future, it is important to be practical. For example, if we were born in the U.S., it would be impractical to visualize becoming the Prime Minister of England.

Or if we were a teenager in the U.S., it would be impractical to visualize becoming the U.S. President before we turned 18.

These sorts of practical realities must be incorporated into our visualizations. We must take a hard look at the time and circumstances of our visualization before we dive into it. Otherwise, the visualization will only lead us into frustration. The teenager who visualized becoming President by age 18, for example, could become depressed once he turned 18 and wasn't anywhere near accomplishing that goal.

Time and Circumstance

Time and circumstance in our visualizations are key components. This is why we are recommending that the specific visualization process take place after the goal-making process for each timeline (Chapters 7 through 10). This will allow us to orchestrate the visualization along the lines of our strategic plan.

In the beginning, we can still broadly visualize our goals. Like the vacation, we can make a general visualization of what it might be like to accomplish a few of our longer-range goals. But then we must look at the realities of the situation and do some specific visualization once the plan is made.

Let's use an example. Let's say that we want to become an Olympic swimmer. Perhaps we might visualize touching the wall in first place. And perhaps we visualize training hard to meet that accomplishment.

These would be appropriate, but let's say that as we complete the goal-making process, we realize that this is not what we want to do as an ultimate career. We realize that becoming an Olympic swimmer is part of our strategic plan but won't be our career. So during our strategic planning process, we incorporate a plan to become an Olympic swimmer during our university years, but then we graduate from university and go on to accomplish our ultimate career goal.

This means that our visualization of our Olympic swimmer days will change. It will now incorporate our being a university student, who eventually graduates and goes on to achieve further accomplishments unrelated to the pool.

This means our visualization of our winning as a swimmer might be founded within university swim meets. This provides us with a more specific visualization—one that gives us a practical goal to accomplish.

We must remember that the more practical and real our visualization is, the more likely we are to accomplish it. And when we accomplish it, we will feel better able to go on to complete other goals in our strategic plan.

While the claim might be, "go with your gut feeling," we can see on a practical basis how visualization leads to accomplishments within ones life journey.

Vision versus Visualization

Visualization is not the same thing as vision.

There are two types of vision. There is anatomical vision and there is philosophical vision. Philosophical vision relates to extending your core values into your plans and actions.

Then there is anatomical vision. Let's review this type of vision for clarity.

Our eyes sense the world around us through the reception, conversion and transmission of waveforms that reflect the visible light portion of the electromagnetic spectrum. The eyes are cylindrical (sinusoidal) with an adjustable lens and shuttering mechanism to focus and limit the entry of light to specific waveforms. The cornea, the aqueous fluid, the iris, pupils, lens, and ciliary muscles all operate in a coordinated fashion to focus on a specific range of wavelengths, frequencies, and amplitudes.

The eyes blink and the pupils contract to filter out waveforms, images, or debris that would otherwise disrupt the images we expect to see. These facilities of the eye are all pre-programmed to accomplish the intentions of the self to see the world in a particular light.

Once the lens mechanics do their work to narrow in on particular waveform ranges, inverted light is filtered through the cornea and lens and inversely reflected onto the retina. The retina is made up of specialized waveform-sensitive receptors. Some one hundred and twenty-five million narrow receptors called *rods* are sensitized to light and darkness.

Another estimated seven million round photoreceptors called *cones* gauge color and depth. The underlying nerve cells use the rods and cones as waveform conversion devices. They effectively translate waveforms of visible light into bioelectromagnetic nerve pulses. These waveforms are conducted through neuron ion channels that provide a pathway through the millions of nerve fibers that make up the optic nerve.

The area where the optic nerve connects to the back of the retina has no rods or cones. This is referred to as the eye's *blind spot* or *optic disc*. To see our blind spot we can simply look at an image with one eye covered and move our perspective until the uncovered eye loses sight of a particular object.

As mentioned, the eyes are trained to pick up specific waveforms of reflected light and not others. They typically do not pick up wavelengths outside of 380 to 760 nanometers. Each type of retinal receptor is also limited in its scope. The rods are sensitive to brightness. They contain a light sensitive photo-pigment called *rhodopsin*. The rods thus respond to lightness or grayness—but not color. Their input is grayscale.

The cones are the color sensor photoreceptors. There are three types of cones: Red cones respond to primarily wavelengths in the red spectrum. Green cones respond primarily to green spectrum wavelengths. Blue cones respond primarily to blue spectrum wavelengths. As a painter's palette may combine these basic three colors to make up the various other colors, wavelengths with different color traits are blended to communicate a particular color.

In the center of the retina is a circular indentation filled with a greater density of cones used for focusing upon brightly lit objects. This is called the *macula*. The macula's cones have direct nerve pathways to the brain when compared to the more spread out rods and cones of the retina.

Thus images received through the macular cones tend to be more distinctive and sharp than images received through the more spread out pigments among the retina. This design allows us to center and fix our eyes upon the visible zones directly in front of our eyes. This allows us to focus upon the views we are most interested in as we turn our heads. Conversely, this focal point allows us to unfocus waveforms for those images we are not particularly interested in.

Our vision is also limited by a number of other factors. Waveforms outside the wavelength range will typically not be converted into impulses. It is unlikely they will even register through the optic nerve mechanism. This is not to say waveforms outside of these wavelengths do not exist or are not visible using the right equipment. The concept of *visible spectrum* is based solely upon our visible range.

The 'visible spectrum' for other organisms differ from that of humans. Human technology has unveiled many other electromagnetic waveform spectra outside the visible spectrum. Even so, most scientists agree that we are still only aware of a tiny sliver of the entire electromagnetic spectrum.

During nerve transmission, visual waveforms also undergo filtration as they are translated through the neurotransmitters within the optic nerve. The chemistry of the neurotransmitter fluid is designed to filter and modulate waveforms, screening out incompatible or unwanted waveforms while leaving others emphasized. Drugs and alcohol can significantly affect the neurotransmitter content, causing an alteration of waveform signals as they pass through the optic nerve.

The intention of the self also affects neurotransmitter content and waveform filtration. The self's subtle programming of the mind modulates the acuity mechanisms of the lens and pupils—as focus is centered upon the subjects that interest us most.

The optic nerve provides the pathway for waveforms translated through the retinal cells to the *lateral geniculate nucleus* (or *LGN*) located within the thalamus. The LGN is made up of a series of bent neuron layers, which alternatively receive visual waveforms through the optic nerve while performing a sorting or integrating function.

Each LGN layer also has a unique combination of cell types, and each cell type appears to process a different part of the information. For example, *parvocellular cells* integrate color and detail about the images, while *magnocellular cells* conduct a short-term integration of images without a lot of detail. *Koniocellular cells,* on the other hand, integrate other sensory information with the images, adding texture or *somato* information.

Research has so far discovered six types of LGN cells, some of which integrate waveforms while others provide cancellation in order to spatially assemble and convert images. Once sorted and converged through the LGN, the resulting waveforms are pulsed to the V1 portion of the visual cortex. Here they interfere with other projecting waveforms to create a mapped screen for the person within to observe.

This last point is important to understand clearly. Individual waveforms reflecting through a specific rod or cone and relayed via the optic nerve have no meaning alone. Rather, it is the converging of multiple waveforms into an interference pattern that projects an image onto the mind.

Without this convergence, there would be no information contained within the image. A single waveform would appear merely as a single band of color and light. We might compare this to looking at one pixel on a computer screen. That one pixel will convey no image in itself.

In other words, vision is a confluence of waveforms driven by the interests of the person within. This confluence creates a total image.

The unmistakable deception our physical eyes present to us is illustrated by the illusion of watching television or cinema. There in front of us, flashing on the screen, is a series of still photographs—each one slightly different from the previous. Each still picture is replaced by another still picture at a rate of some twenty-four frames per second. In comparison, our eyes, LGN, visual cortex and mind can only process at a rate of about fifty or sixty images per second.

As a result, while our eyes and minds are perceiving one photograph, another is flashed. This blurs the two images together, giving us the false impression of movement. We fail to see that about half the time we spend watching TV or a movie we are actually looking at a blank screen.

The bottom line is that seeing is not actually taking place within any of the anatomy. The eyes, optic nerve and brain are simply transmitters—like an antenna and video terminal. All of these instruments merely receive, convert and relay informational waveforms of particular specification.

Once the information waves pass through the optic nerve they are mapped through the visual cortex and reflected interactively among neurons that resonate with those waveforms. These interactive waveform reflections create a sort of mental mapping system. This mapping creates a holographic 'screen-shot' of the image onto the mind. This facsimile of the image might be compared to a scan or copy.

The act of seeing is quite different from this holographic screen shot. *Seeing* is what takes place by a *seer*. Seeing thus requires consciousness—someone who is aware—observing what the neurons are flashing upon the screen of the mind. Moreover, the equipment this conscious seer utilizes is not absolute. The seer thus can adjust the foci of the senses to perceive what is most beneficial to the objectives of the seer.

It thus appears that vision and color are not as simple as we might think. Vision provides a waveform bridge between the physical world and the conscious self. What we decide to look at and reflect upon truly affects our consciousness, just as our consciousness affects what we perceive and take away from what we look at. It is a cycle of awareness and perception steeped in consciousness.

The same seer—the person within—can also manipulate stored images and project them upon our mind's screen. The trick here is that the seer can give the same 'reality' to a stored image as it can one coming in from the LGN. This gives us the ability to paint our own reality, using visualization techniques.

But we have to be careful when using visualization. Because of this ability to paint our own reality, we can also miss much of what is going on around us. This has the danger of giving us an altered view of reality, which isn't good.

To some degree, most of us have altered views of reality, however. For example, two people attending the same event may recall two entirely different versions of the event. In the same way, we each have distinctly different recognition levels due to our expectations of the world around us.

It is when we communicate and compare what we think we see that we gain a consensus view. Sometimes this occurs after the event. Other times it may occur instantly, as we look around us for other's responses. As most of us seek the love and acceptance of others, we tend to quickly inherit a collective vision.

Stepping Away from Collective Vision

In order to embark on a future that departs from our previous expectations or the expectations of family members or peers, we may need to step away from the collective view of those around us.

This may or may not be necessary, depending upon the collective view of those around us, and whether or not that collective vision inhibits us from achieving our Plan for Life.

Stepping away from such a collective view can be done through the self-discovery process and Plan for Life process proposed in this book.

This is distinct from what some might consider a rebellion of convention. It is actually quite easy to become a rebel. A rebel is focused upon rejecting the vision of others. The rebellion of convention means to strike out on our own and establish our own vision of our life.

Our Plan for Life is intended to build something new. Something unique to us. Something that no one has ever done before. And something that no one will ever do like we do it.

Coloring our Visualizations

As we visualize our Plan for Life, we can use colors to cement our missions and vision into goals. This subtle painting of our mindscreen with color provokes messaging that we can reflect upon for years to come.

Why? Because colors affect our emotions. And our emotions create the textures that link up our mind with the specific missions and goals that we set up for our visualization.

We can compare this technique to remembering names. What is the best way to remember a person's name? To make up a visualization that creates a mental link between the name and a visual impression. For example, we can remember the name Fred by imagining that our new acquaintance plays basketball with a big red ball. Then we can imagine Fred playing with a red ball.

By imagining Fred playing with a red ball, we bring into our mind a visualization with a color. This color will attach our mindscreen's image of the color with the name.

In the same way, we can not only create our visualizations in color: We can use those colors to help us cement our goals into our future.

The secret to this technique lies in the fact that different colors affect our cognition, moods and behavior in different ways. Brain imaging research has illustrated these differences. Different colors stimulate corresponding brainwave patterns. And each of these brainwave patterns are linked with particular moods and behaviors.

The mechanism for this subtle electromagnetic bridge is explainable using wave resonance and interference models. Touching a piano key in a room full of pianos would cause the other pianos to vibrate in the same chord.

With color resonance, we can associate particular waveforms with other waveform patterns occurring within the body. These waveforms stimulate internal waveform responses.

The longer wavelengths of red colors stimulate higher frequency beta waves in the brain at more than thirteen cycles per second and wavelengths of 630-700 nanometers. Red colors tend to stimulate autonomic systems, increasing heart rate and blood pressure. Red also stimulates circulation, hostility, violence, jealousy and competition.

Orange stimulates high alpha brainwaves between ten cycles and thirteen cycles per second at wavelengths of

590 to 630 nanometers. Orange also stimulates energy similar to red, but without some of the heat or intensity that red brings. Orange is warming. It tends to encourage enthusiasm, creativity, inquisitiveness, sincerity, thoughtfulness, and decongesting effects.

Yellow stimulates lower alpha brainwaves at eight or nine cycles per second with wavelengths of 560 to 590 nanometers. Yellow resonates with spontaneity, compassion, memory, learning, and appetite. It stimulates the stomach, upper intestines and the adrenal glands.

Yellow can thus trigger stress in certain situations. Because yellow reflects light with a greater intensity, it can tire the eyes and mind after some time. Activities associated with yellow include memorization, study, and focus. Yellow can be cheerful, but this can also lead to fatigue with an overload. Research has illustrated that babies tend to cry more and couples tend to argue more in yellow rooms.

Green stimulates higher theta region brainwaves at six to seven cycles per second with wavelengths of 490 to 560 nanometers. Green is calming, balancing, healing, soothing and invigorating. It stimulates growth, love and a sense of security. Green resonates with devotion, caring and giving.

Green stimulates healing, particularly related to the cardiovascular system and lungs. Green has been shown to stimulate the immune system. Increased T-cell levels have been observed. Green tends to suppress the body's endogenous melatonin, aiding the body to cool down, relax and sleep. Green also stimulates problem solving, negotiation and resolution.

Blue stimulates lower theta waves in the five to six cycles per second at wavelengths of 450 to 490 nanometers. Blue is cooling, calming and stable. Blue is associated with the lungs, breathing, sound, and thyroid function. As the thyroid is part of the temperature regulating system, it helps stabilize core body temperature and the cellular metabolism rates.

Blue stimulates creativity and communication. Blue also stimulates detoxification and purification systems within the body. Blue is a very good color for over-active children and stressed situations, because it tends to calm and relax the mind.

Indigo stimulates low delta waves around one cycle per second at wavelengths of 400 to 450 nanometers. It is often considered the color of the 'third eye.'

Indigo is associated with clarity, decision-making, leadership and intelligence. The sinuses, vision, and the immune system are stimulated by and resonate with indigo. Activities most associated with indigo would be highly intellectual activity, humanitarian behavior, medical research, and philosophical contemplation.

Violet stimulates higher delta waves from two to four cycles per second—slightly faster than indigo. Violet waves are associated with the seventh *chakra* region. Violet is associated with consciousness and intuition. It is a color linked with personal growth and learning. It is also associated with brain circulation, spinal fluid movement, and joint fluids. Violet activities are associated with inspiration, prayer, and spiritual insight.

Certain blended colors have yet their own unique effects. Pink has been associated with tranquilizing, sedative and muscle-relaxing effects, for example. Notably, Dr.

Alexander Schauss reported in his color research that these same effects occurred among colorblind patients.

Color pigments are also nutritional and therapeutic in foods. Lycopene, curcumin, carotenes, rhodospsin, lutein, canthaxanthin, zeaxanthins, sulforaphanes, isoiocyanates, anthocyanidins, pomeratrol, pycnogenol, and other poly-phenols all contribute to giving botanicals color. These pigments also provide cancer prevention, antioxidant activity and various other nutritional benefits.

So how can we affect our visualizations using colors? First, by putting ourselves in an environment that reflects the colors we seek to visualize.

In most cases, this means sitting down in a natural environment, with natural lighting. If we sit in a forest or park setting, we'll have plenty of natural green colors present. We can sit next to a garden of flowers to absorb other colors. We can sit next to a sunset to receive some yellow and orange colors. We can sit next to the ocean to get blue colors. We can also lay on our back in the park and look up at the sky to receive blue colors.

As we look around our natural environment to receive these colors, we can then close our eyes to visualize our future. Our mindscreen will automatically integrate the colors we see around us into the visualization.

Once we have established the right environment and setting to conduct our visualization, we can follow some basic techniques to accomplish a full visualization of our future.

Achieving Alpha Brainwaves

Now let's discuss the mechanical techniques of visualization. The fundamental technique for visualization calls for arriving at a state of mental relaxation. This means creating a peak in our alpha brainwaves.

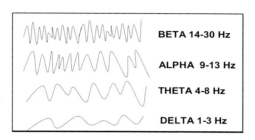

What are brainwaves? These are oscillations of electrical current between our various neurons. Our brainwaves reflect our thought processing and level of cognition.

Most of our waking life, our brains cycle with beta waves, at fourteen to thirty cycles per second (hertz). Beta waves are dominant during active thinking and problem solving. These waves tend to be prominent towards the front of the brain—where the frontal cortex is located—and on the sides—where the motor cortices are located. Beta waves reflect a state of focused attention.

Gamma waves have higher frequencies, and are sometimes referred to as high-frequency beta waves. Gamma waves predominate during intense problem solving and focused learning. Gamma waves range from thirty to sixty hertz. Gamma waves occur during increased visual cortex activity and the brain's sorting processes. Higher gamma brainwaves—cycling from sixty to two hundred hertz, can also occur during intense cognitive brain functions.

The alpha brainwave state occurs when we are awake but in a more clear-headed but meditative state. Alpha waves range from eight to thirteen hertz. Alpha waves will predominate when we are calm, relaxed and yet still alert. Alpha waves can also occur when we are in a state of focused learning. Alpha waves have been seen during meditative exercises such as Tai chi, Yoga and Qigong.

Shortly we will discuss some specific techniques to achieve an alpha brainwave state for our visualizations.

Delta waves are slower, longer brainwaves that range from a half to three hertz.. These will occur when we are lightly sleeping (dreamless) or during deep meditative states. During the delta brainwaves our awareness of the external environment becomes suspended. Therefore, while delta waves are good for relaxation and meditation, this state is not conducive to visualization techniques. Why? Because we need to be in more control of our visualizations.

Theta brainwaves are a little faster than delta waves, at three to eight cycles per second. These brainwaves will predominate during deep sleep, often when we are dreaming. During theta waves, we are completely removed from the physical realities around us. We are seeing the world within our minds and possibly beyond during this state.

For those of us who develop a good meditative discipline to promote alpha brainwaves during our visualizations, we might occasionally fall into some theta brainwave cycles. These might be accompanied by a reverie about our future. This can be good as long as we have the discipline to keep it practical and doable.

The Visualization Environment

We discussed this with respect to color, but our environment can help encourage an alpha brainwave state.

That is, what we see, hear, smell and feel. The best environment to achieve alpha brainwaves is a natural and quiet setting, surrounded by natural colors. The more variety of natural colors the better, because these will stimulate our emotional ties to our visualization. Here is a list of potential environments that will help us achieve an alpha brainwave state:

- A forest
- A large park
- A quite beach
- A rowboat on a lake
- A sailboat in the ocean

If we cannot easily find one of these, then we can at least find a small park at a very quiet time of day. The reason "large park" is specified above is because many city parks—especially small parks—can be particularly noisy. In these we can be disturbed by car noise, yelling, music, barbeques and so on.

These disturbances not only prevent the alpha state. They can also interfere in our visualization process. Anything that creates imaging or sensual experience related to society can disturb not just the visualization process—but the achievement of those goals that we are setting up to accomplish.

Our Seating Arrangement

Next we need to find a comfortable seat or seating position. Depending upon our condition, we can choose from a variety of seats:

- Cross-legged (or lotus) sitting posture on soft grass or on a cushion
- Knees folded with our back reclined on a tree or rock (a cushion might help too)
- Comfortable lawn chair
- A park bench (again, a cushion can help)

These are only examples. The environment we pick will to some degree dictate our choice of seats. The bottom line is to choose a position that allows us to straighten our back and breathe deeply.

When sitting for deep breathing, the lower back can be arched slightly with the upper spine fairly straight and relaxed, with the back of the head in line with our lower spine. We can sit on the front of our 'sit bones' at the base of the pelvis, rather than the backside of our sit bones where the lower spine tends to curve outward. When we are sitting on the right part of our sit bones, our lower back will naturally arch.

Lying down is specifically discouraged for visualization. This can inevitably lead to falling asleep during the process. Especially when we incorporate slow breathing into the process.

The combination of sitting position, environment and breathing correctly will help us accomplish the alpha brain wave state. Let's learn (or relearn) to breathe, in order to get to alpha:

Deep Breathing

Deep breathing is one of the best ways to increase both lung capacity and respiration efficiency. This is because it strengthens and enlarges the diaphragm, strengthens the supporting abdominal muscles, relaxes the smooth muscles of the airways, and helps reduce stress.

We will discuss a number of methods here, but we focus on two established techniques for healthy deep breathing:

- Slowly push out the abdomen around the belly button. As the lungs fill, push out the upper abdomen. You can test this by watching or feeling the abdomen rise.
- Continue pushing the abdomen out until the abdomen is comfortably fully pushed out.
- Top it off by expanding the rib cage to completely fill the tops of the lungs.
- Hold in position and relax for 3-7 seconds.
- Then push the air out by slowly contracting the upper abdominal muscles followed by contracting the lower abdomen as the lungs are completely emptied. This last step is called flooring.

As we breathe in, we can look around us and absorb the nature around us. As we breathe out, we can breathe away the petty concerns of our current situation. We can breathe away those issues relating to money, job, time and people who need one thing or another from us.

Then we can breathe in the colors of our environment and with each breath, breathe out the day-to-day details of our life.

After soaking in the natural setting and breathing deeply, we should soon accomplish the alpha brain wave state. Then we can close our eyes and begin to visualize our future.

How do we know we've achieved the alpha state? We don't necessarily have to know for sure. But if we are able to unfocus our mind from our day-to-day details and breathe in the colors of our natural environment, we should be close enough to alpha.

Visualization Techniques

Once the relaxed state of primarily alpha brainwaves is arrived at, we can begin to visualize the accomplishment of our goals.

The basic techniques utilize a stepped process:

1. Deciding on the goals (the strategic plan)
2. Arriving at a relaxed state of mind
3. Envisioning our future environment
4. Seeing ourselves accomplishing the goal(s)
5. Taking a snapshot (still) upon our mindscreen of our favorite image of ourselves accomplishing the goal(s)
6. Switching our visual from the first party view (as we would see it) to a third party view (as others would see it).
7. Visualize the benefits related to accomplishing our goal(s)
8. Feeling the accomplishment as we visualize that future environment
9. Focusing on achieving the goal(s)
10. Becoming comfortable with our accomplishment. This means seeing some portion of our day-to-day life after we've accomplished the goal.

Visualizing the Details

Visualizing the accomplishment of our goals means visualizing the details along with the broad brushes. Once we can put our mind's eye into the situation by visualizing the details, we will be able to unlock the power of visualization.

Visualizing the details means focusing our mind upon the small things within the vision. The more details we visualize, the more real the visualization becomes to our subconscious. This effects our mind the same way that vision effects the eyes. The details picked up by the optic nerve are filled in by the mind, which makes the image seem real.

In the same way, when we visualize the details, our mind fills in the blanks. This helps encourage the mind to accept the vision of the future as reality as opposed to hope.

When the mind is encouraged to accept the visualization as reality, the subconscious mind begins to work in subtle ways to achieve those objectives visualized. This is a potent part of the process.

Because these are powerful techniques, it is critical to carefully develop our goals before we dive into visualization. We'll do this at each step of our strategic planning process.

Yes, the process of developing our plan will utilize some special visualization techniques. These will help us activate our personal strategic plan.

Chapter Seven

Your Lifetime Objectives

Now that we've done a some self-discovery, done a personal inventory, and created a mission statement and vision statement, we should now have a clearer picture of what we have to work with and what direction we are headed in general.

By, 'what we have to work with' I mean your situation. Your strengths and weaknesses. Your passions. Your spiritual values, mission and vision about your life.

We have compartmentalized these into relevant categories:

- Body: Physical and environmental goals
- Mind: Cognitive, emotional, intellectual goals
- Spirit: Spiritual goals
- Career: Occupational goals
- Social: Family, community goals

Using the goals and objectives worksheet: Start with the lifetime timeline. Next to each category item, make a list of things you want to accomplish in your lifetime.

Make sure that all of your lifetime goals align with your mission and vision statements. They need to be cohesive and compatible.

In other words, your lifetime goals should fully execute your mission and vision. While a short-term set of goals may require you to accomplish intermediate steps, the lifetime goals should fully address your mission.

Also be sure that your timeline makes sense. The lifetime objectives need to be things that are accomplished at some point in your lifetime. They can include things accomplished in five or ten years, for example. But they must be practical things you aim to accomplish. They cannot be things that might occur after your lifetime is over, or things that others will do for you. They have to be things that you will personally accomplish.

Your lifetime goals should also assume that the preliminary goals are accomplished. For example, if your lifetime goal includes becoming a judge, then it is okay to exclude the goal of graduating from law school. The lifetime goal of becoming a judge would require graduating from law school. But this is to be assumed in earlier goals.

At the same time, you can still include preliminary goals in your lifetime set of goals if you want. But this may serve to confuse your visualization process. It might signal to your mind that it would be fine if you just got through law school and didn't become a judge. So it's better to include the preliminary goals within those timelines that you seek to accomplish those.

Take some time to complete this. Take a few days or a week. Fill out a few parts each day, and sleep on it. You can do this on the computer so you can easily erase what you aren't comfortable with. Be sure that you can live with your goals. Think carefully about this. Don't short-change yourself. Be lofty.

At the same time, be reasonable. Write down goals that you want to achieve that are doable. Be careful of impossible goals that will only frustrate you later.

Visualize your Lifetime Goals

Once you have completed this lifetime timeline goals list, take your lifetime timeline goals list and go to a quiet place in a natural setting as described in the last chapter.

Breathe deeply and slowly from the abdomen. Enter into a state of relaxation as we discussed in the visualization chapter.

Close your eyes and watch the screen of your mind. Imagine yourself achieving your lifetime goals on your timeline.

Now visualize having accomplished each of these lifetime goals one by one. Paint your mindscreen with the time and circumstance of having accomplished each of those goals.

Go back in time and see yourself achieving each of your lifetime goals, one at a time.

With each accomplishment, look around you at the details of your surroundings as you see yourself accomplish each goal. For some, you can combine goals into one imagination setting. Whatever feels most comfortable.

Now look through a third-party's eyes and see yourself accomplishing each goal. Again, look around at the details as described in the visualization module.

After you have imagined accomplishing each goal individually, imagine yourself having accomplished all the goals at once. Look at your environment and surroundings as you have accomplished these.

This would mean seeing yourself during your later years. Look in the mirror on your mindscreen. Visualize your body as it is older. Your body may have grey hair now, for example. Visualize some other details about yourself. Now see yourself in light of having accomplished your goals already.

Now see yourself having accomplished your goals through a third party having accomplished these goals. You can choose a trusted person—someone that you feel will be there when you accomplish these things. This may be a spouse, or sibling. Or you can choose someone of the public who may be observing you having accomplished your goals.

As you visualize these goals, you can assess whether they are congruent for you. If you feel odd when you visualize yourself having accomplished any goal, stop and think about it: Does this goal really fit with your mission? Are you really passionate about this goal? Are you trying to achieve this goal for others or yourself?

If you are trying to achieve a goal for others—the symptom will be that you will easily be able to visualize yourself as a third party, but will have difficulty visualizing yourself having completed the goal as yourself. You'll feel a bit strange. Investigate this feeling. Go deeper and figure out why you are not feeling right about this goal.

This doesn't have to be answered in one sitting. If you feel strange but aren't sure why, then stop the visualization process and return to your daily activities—but think about why visualizing that goal might have bothered you. It might take you a few days to realize what the problem is. Don't rush this process. Take at least a week to complete this exercise.

Make sure you are comfortable with your Plan for Life visualization. If you aren't, then make some changes to the plan and repeat the visualization process. During the next visualization, try changing some of the details of the visualization. For example, you might consider changing the venue where you achieve the goals. Or the second- and third-parties that see you achieve these.

Exercises:

Consider someone you admire. This could be a historic person or a person in your family. Now imagine they were your age, and they are constructing their lifetime goals. What would they list? Try to list out what they might have listed out as their lifetime goals.

Your Life Plan
Goals and Objectives Worksheet
Name:
Date:

Goal Setting:

	Body: *Physical status, living condition, location, etc.*	**Mind:** *Mental status, cognitive relationships, emotional well-being*	**Spirit:** *Spiritual status and growth, activities that promote spirit well-being*	**Career:** *Occupational and financial goals that relate to work and monetization*	**Social:** *Goals related to family and community*
Lifetime Goals					
Twenty Year Goals					
Ten Year Goals					
Five Year Goals					
One Year Goals					
Short-term Goals Term: _____					

Chapter Eight

Your 20-Year and 10-Year Plan

Now that you've completed your lifetime goals, you should now develop a clear picture of what you need to accomplish within 20 years and 10 years in order to accomplish those lifetime goals.

This means looking at the specifics of each goal, and determining what has to happen before you can achieve each. This might mean gaining a certain degree or position, or perhaps a particular pattern or lifestyle.

This will lead you to developing what we might call "sub-goals." That is, requirements that will allow you to achieve your lifetime goals.

Again, compartmentalize each sub-goal into relevant categories:

- Body: Physical and environmental goals
- Mind: Cognitive, emotional, intellectual goals
- Spirit: Spiritual goals
- Career: Occupational goals
- Social: Family, community goals

Using the goals and objectives worksheet: Start with the 20-year timeline. Next to this timeline, list out each goal you will need to accomplish in order to complete the lifetime goals in that category.

If you have other goals that you want to accomplish in this period that aren't in the lifetime goal, then add these. Then consider whether you want to now add them to the lifetime goals timeline as well.

Make sure these timeline sub-goals also align with your mission and vision statements. You don't want to stray from your mission, vision and core values in order to achieve your lifetime goals. It is not as though you have to sacrifice one for the other. If you do, then you need to revisit your mission, vision and lifetime goals.

And be sure that your timeline makes sense. Make sure it's reasonable that you can accomplish those sub-goals in 20 years and 10 years respectively.

Visualize Your 20- and 10-year Goals

Complete the 20-year plan and visualize that before you list out your 10-year plan. For each, enter into a state of relaxation as we discussed in the last module. Take your list of goals and complete the process of visualization as described in the previous chapter.

Again, visualize accomplishing each goal by seeing your environment and noticing the details. Then see yourself accomplishing each goal as a third party looking on.

Now see yourself at 20 years having already accomplished all those goals. Look at some of the details. Now see yourself as a third party having accomplished those goals.

Assuming you are comfortable with the visualization, you can proceed to completing the 10-year plan and repeat the process. However, it is advisable to take a couple of days to digest your 20-year plan before you start on your 10-year plan. Make sure you are comfortable with your visualization. If you aren't, then make some changes to the plan and repeat the visualization.

When you are comfortable, take your 10-year timeline goals list and go to a quiet place in a natural setting and breathe deeply and slowly from the abdomen again. Close your eyes and imagine yourself achieving the 10-year goals on your timeline.

See yourself accomplishing each goal. Look around you at the details of your surroundings as you accomplish this goal. Now look through a third-party's eyes and see yourself accomplishing this goal. Again, look around at the details as described in the visualization module.

Again, as you visualize these goals, you are assessing whether they fit. If you feel uncomfortable when you visualize yourself accomplishing any goal, stop and think about it: Does this goal fit with your mission? Are you really passionate about this goal? Are you trying to achieve this goal for others or yourself?

Remember, if you are trying to achieve a goal for others—you will easily be able to visualize yourself as a third party, but will have difficulty visualizing yourself completing the goal in the first person. You'll feel a bit strange. Investigate this feeling. Go deeper and figure out why you are not feeling right about this goal.

This doesn't have to be answered in one sitting. If you feel strange but aren't sure why, then stop the visualization process and return to your daily activities—but thinking about why visualizing that goal might have bothered you.

Also it might help to watch your dreams for the next few days. Our dreams often tell us what we are truly comfortable with. But be careful as dreams can also deceive us with pipe dreams and illusions.

Exercise:
Again consider someone you admire. This could be a historic person or a person in your family. Now imagine what their sub-goals would have to have been in order for them to have accomplished what they accomplished in life. Try to list what these sub-goals for 10 and 20 years might have been.

Chapter Nine

Your 5-Year and 1-Year Plan

Now that we've completed our 10-year goals, we should now develop a clear understanding of what we need to do within the next five years to accomplish those goals. Once we have these five year goals set, we can then set goals for the next year.

These might be considered sub-goals as well, but some goals may be lifetime goals if we can accomplish them during one of these timelines.

Now compartmentalize each goal into relevant categories using the worksheet:

- Body: Physical and environmental goals
- Mind: Cognitive, emotional, intellectual goals
- Spirit: Spiritual goals
- Career: Occupational goals
- Social: Family, community goals

As we did with the 20-year and 10-year goals, use the goals and objectives worksheet and start with the 5-year timeline. Next to this timeline item, list out each goal in each category that you will need to accomplish in order to complete the 10-year goals in that category.

If you have other goals that you want to accomplish in this period that isn't in the 10-year goals, add it, but again consider whether it makes sense to add it to the 10-year, 20-year and lifetime goals timelines.

Once again, make sure these timeline goals align with your mission and vision statements. Be sure your timeline makes sense. You don't want to be too aggressive. If you are too aggressive you may not be able to reach your five year goals. If you can't reach those, your other goal timelines may be in danger. Remember your self-discovery process we discussed earlier. Remember your assets and liabilities. If you need to develop more assets to accomplish your five-year goals, make sure that you allow for that in your five-year timeline goals. Achieving those assets will then become part of the five-year list of goals.

If you feel a need to put a timeline between the one and five year timelines, feel free to do this. This is your plan. You should feel comfortable with it.

Again, once you have completed your five-year plan, enter into your state of relaxation as we discussed in the last module. Take your five-year list first and do this. Complete the process of visualization. Five years out shouldn't be too hard to visualize. Take your current environment and expand that to five years in order to visualize it.

Notice the changes that you see taking place in five years. Maybe you've moved. Maybe you have a job in five years that you don't have now. Maybe you have lost some weight or gotten married. See these changes in detail. Breathe in the colors of your environment to see these changes on your mindscreen.

Now see yourself in the first person accomplishing each of your goals. Now see yourself in the third person doing the same.

Now see yourself having accomplished all of your goals at five years. See from the first person and then through a third person. It really doesn't matter who that third person is. It could be a spectator or a spouse. You choose.

Assuming you are comfortable, proceed to the one-year plan. List out all your timeline goals and repeat the visualization process. The one-year plan should be very practical and should include things that you should easily be able to accomplish within the year.

This is where practical conservatism will really benefit you. If you are too optimistic, you might miss these goals. That will endanger your five-year plan.

Again, take your one-year timeline goals list and go to your quiet place in a natural setting and repeat the visualization process. The one-year goals will be more easily to visualize because many things won't change for you within the year. Perhaps you'll be living in the same place. Perhaps you will achieve your goals at the same school or job that you are working at now. Or maybe something will change. See that change specifically by noticing the details surrounding the change. If it is a change of school, visualize a class in the new school, or learning a specific subject.

Visualize all these as you are accomplishing your goals, along with those things that will change during the year.

Again, as you visualize these goals, make sure they fit and feel comfortable. Sometimes our longer-range goals will become suspicious when our short-term goals don't make sense to us. So be ready to adjust your longer-range goals as you assess and visualize your shorter-term goals.

Remember to stop and consider: Does each goal fit with my mission and core values? Am I really passionate about this? Am I trying to achieve this for others or myself?

Again, these questions don't have to be answered in one sitting. If you feel uncomfortable about anything, stop the visualization process and think about it for a few days. Sleep on it. Dream on it.

Exercise:

If you are comfortable, share at least one of your five-year and one-year goals with someone you trust. If you are not comfortable sharing any of your goals, then list what might have been a one-year goal of a famous person you admire.

Chapter Ten

Your Short-Term Plan

Our one-year goal will feed into our short-term goals. Do we need shorter-term goals than one year? This completely depends upon the type of goals we project for the one year plan.

I would recommend at least a 90-day plan to cover some of the short-term elements that are necessary to put in place to achieve your one-year plan. Now if you want you can also do a six-month plan. Or instead of the 90-day plan, do a six-month plan.

For the sake of this discussion, let's assume you are implementing a 90-day plan. This gets you from zero to mach one speed towards achieving your goals. It sets you up to achieve your one-year goals. So this is extremely important.

This also means the 90-day plan gets into some details. Start with where your life is now. Look at your one-year goals. What practical things do you have to put in place to achieve these?

I can tell you from experience: If you don't do this, you can end up halfway through the year realizing you are not tracking towards your one-year goals. This will mess up your entire life plan and discourage you.

What I mean by details: We're talking about the ugly stuff of everyday life. Getting registered. Getting permission. Signing up for something. Establishing your place within whatever is needed to get those goals done.

It also may require some arrangements of money. Or arrangements with people. Or parents. Or kids. Whatever is needed on the mundane level should be put into the 90-day plan.

Again, these need to be compartmentalized into the relevant categories:

- Body: Physical and environmental goals
- Mind: Cognitive, emotional, intellectual goals
- Spirit: Spiritual goals
- Career: Occupational goals
- Social: Family, community goals

As we did with the longer-term goals, use the same goals and objectives worksheet. Next to the 90-day timeline item, list out each goal in each category that you will need to accomplish in order to complete the one-year goals in that category.

If you have other requirements that you have to get done that don't affect the one-year plan, you should still add these. Some of these might mean 'clearing the decks' so to speak.

Again, be sure these timeline goals align with your mission and vision statements. Make sure your timeline makes sense. You need to be practical. If you realize you can't get everything done to match the one-year goals, go back and adjust the goals in previous timelines. Make sure you can achieve those things you list.

Remember the self-discovery process, and your assets and liabilities. You might want to update this personal inventory with skills or weaknesses as you realize them on a practical level.

In addition to the Life goals worksheet, I have attached another sheet specifically for the short-term plan at the end of this chapter. This allows you to put in your short-term goals on one sheet with achievement dates.

The reason for this is that short-term plans often can be achieved at different times. For example, a goal to get registered in a particular school might only take a week, while another goal might take a month. So it makes sense to attach a goal timeline to each short-term goal.

Next to the "Goal Date" column is the "Date Achieved." This allows you to put in the date you achieved your goal. This of course allows you to track whether you achieved this particular goal. It also allows you to test your sense of timeline: Are you pretty accurate in estimating how long you will take to achieve something?

If you aren't, that's fine. You simply have to adjust your timelines as needed.

Now once you have completed this short-term plan, enter into your state of relaxation as discussed in the previous chapter. Take the short-term list and complete the process of visualization.

Take your short-term timeline goals and go to your quiet place in a natural setting and repeat the visualization process. Match your short-term goals with your one-year goals, and visualize yourself completing each goal. The details will be easier for you to notice. Take your current environment and place within it those things that would change as you accomplish each goal.

See how achieving these will change things around you. This should be much easier to visualize yourself accomplishing these goals, as the next few weeks unwind.

Again, make sure these all fit your lifestyle (or lifestyle changes) and feel comfortable to you.

Remember to ask yourself: Does each goal fit your mission? Are you really passionate about this completing these? Are you trying to achieve this for others or yourself? Yes, some of these short-term tasks might feel mundane. But they should not lie outside of your core values and mission.

Take a week or so to answer these questions. If you feel uncomfortable about anything, stop the visualization process and think about it for a few days.

Exercise: If you are comfortable, share at least one of your short-term goals with another member of this class. If you are not comfortable sharing any of your goals, then share what would have been a goal of a famous person you admire.

Exercise:

If you are comfortable, share at least one of your short-term goals with someone you trust. If you are not comfortable sharing any of your goals, then list what might have been a short-term goal of a famous person you admire.

YOUR SHORT-TERM PLAN

Your LifePlan - Short-term Plan

Name: _____

Dates from/to: _____

Goals	Month One	Month Three	Month Three	Month Four	Month Five	Month Six
Body						
Mind						
Spirit						
Career						
Social						

Chapter Eleven

Assessing Your Plan

Meeting your goals requires a clear tracking system. Sure, you can set your goals down in writing and then just look back to see if you accomplished these or not. That is better than nothing.

But a better system would be to develop a scoring system that allows you to not simply assess whether you have achieved your goals: But a system that also allows you to grade yourself.

Okay, just think about this carefully. Let's say that you set up a goal that you are going to get through a course within a month. So you look at the course and you divide it up into accomplishments within each of four weeks. Now at the end of the first week, instead of getting through a quarter of the course, you only get through a fifth of it. How will you grade yourself for this goal?

Certainly, you won't give yourself 10 points out of 10. Perhaps 7 or 8, depending upon how you far you got through the course.

This type of grading system allows you to assess yourself on a more accurate basis. You can also count your grades over a whole range of goals. This will allow you to not only see how well you are doing in general. It can allow you to see how well you are at setting goals. It can also allow you to see which types of goals you are most inclined to achieve.

You see, many of us will set up goals that we think we want to achieve. But on a daily basis, we find ourselves not progressing towards achieving these goals. Why?

This is something we have to figure out. We might assume that we are simply just a little lazy.

Or perhaps something else is going on.

Let's say, for example, that we are scoring well on achieving several goals, but we are lagging in achieving one particular goal. This could be that we are more challenged in the skills that help us achieving this particular goal.

This means that we need to possibly push back the dates on that particular goal, and add some time to strengthen ourselves with regard to those challenges. This basically simply means adjusting our timelines and perhaps adding an intermediate goal or two. It doesn't have to mean abandoning the goal.

In the example above about the course you thought you would finish in a month, after two weeks of slower-than-planned progression, you might consider giving that course two months to complete instead of a month.

It is also possible that our slower-than-expected progress might mean something else. It might mean that perhaps we are just not that passionate about achieving that particular goal. Perhaps we are not tracking well on that goal because it doesn't tie well into our mission statement. Or perhaps the aspect of our mission statement that ties into this goal doesn't feel that right to us after all. We might just have to make some significant adjustments to our goals.

This illustrates how we can use a scoring system to not just see if we are meeting our goals. We can also use it to assess ourselves about whether we are truly comfortable with those goals and/or timelines.

At the end of this chapter I have included a split-up form providing a scoring system you can use for this purpose:

Weekly Goal Assessment

This form is set up to help us track our one-year goals, but it can be used to track our progress on any of our goals.

On the left column you can list your goals. Then each week you can put in your assessment scores on a 1-10 basis. If you are tracking well towards a particular goal that week, you can mark this with a 10. If you did nothing, you can mark this with a 0. Or you can grade yourself somewhere in between if you did something but aren't tracking 100% towards achieving that goal.

It is not as though every week you will have to achieve something for every goal. Some goals may not have activity in a particular week. If that's the case, you can still give yourself a "10" for that week, assuming you knew you didn't or couldn't do anything that particular week.

Now you can add your total scores each week, and also add your scores at the end of the year towards your goal. Again, these totals help you assess yourself. They allow you to track but also understand whether you have set your goals right. So don't be afraid to total these up each week and give yourself a review.

It's probably not a great idea to adjust your goals in the first week, but you should start to see patterns after about a month. Those goals you are not tracking well towards should be looked at carefully. You don't want to wait too long to begin adjusting your goals or your goal timeline.

Your Life Plan
Weekly Goal Assessment

Name: _____

Begin Date: _____

Goal	Activity Basis	Point Scale	1	2	3	4	5	6	7	8	9	10	11	12	13	14	15	16
Body		0-10																
		0-10																
		0-10																
		0-10																
		0-10																
Mind		0-10																
		0-10																
		0-10																
		0-10																
		0-10																
		0-10																
Spirit		0-10																
		0-10																
		0-10																
		0-10																
		0-10																
		0-10																
Career		0-10																
		0-10																
		0-10																
		0-10																
		0-10																
		0-10																
Social		0-10																
		0-10																
		0-10																
		0-10																
		0-10																
		0-10																
TOTAL POINTS																		

17	18	19	20	21	22	23	24	25	26	27	28	29	30	31	32	33	34	35	36	37

38	39	40	41	42	43	44	45	46	47	48	49	50	51	52	TOTAL

Chapter Twelve

Your Plan for Departure

Our Plan for Life has allowed us to make a cohesive plan to accomplish our goals. However, our plan is incomplete without a plan for our departure.

The reality is, every body will die at some point. There is no getting around this fact. There is nothing morose about this because it is the reality of our situation. Yes, we will have to leave behind our loved ones. But they will also depart at some point too, maybe even ahead of us. And there is clear evidence that we will rejoin them at some point in the future.

Yes, death can come as a surprise. No one knows the exact time or circumstance in which we will leave this earth. But we can know with certainty that we will leave. And we can have some forethought so there is a plan in place for this departure.

Planning for this departure means that when that time comes, we will be better prepared to face it.

Quite simply, death is a normal phase of the body. It has the same importance that birth has. Death arrives at a time when the body is naturally becoming obsolete. As designed, the inner self exits when a significant portion of the body's major functions or organs break down.

This is to our benefit. If we had to wait for all the parts of the body to break down before leaving, we would experience a greater amount of suffering. Instead, as soon as any of the major body parts—such as the heart, liver, kidneys, brain and so on—shuts down, the self is immediately escorted out of the body.

In this chapter we will discuss how to plan for our departure. We will also discuss how to delay our departure to the extent naturally possible. And we will also discuss how we can keep our wits about us as long as possible—potentially staving off the potential for Alzheimer's and other forms of dementia in our later years. This will not only stave off our departure: It will also give us a better shot at achieving all of our goals and objectives in life.

Delaying our Departure

As far as diseases go, the number one cause of death in modern civilization has been heart disease, followed by cancer. Heart disease is a result of the modern diet. Over the past few years, cancer has overtaken heart disease as the leading killer.

Higher cancer rates have been connected to the chemical revolution of the past fifty years. And heart disease deaths have been linked to diet. Prevention strategies are thus clear and well-researched.

Due to the prevention education efforts and research focus of the American Heart Association and the American Cancer Society, death from these two diseases have been slightly decreasing, while their occurrence appears to be continuing to increase.

We might attribute the lower heart disease and cancer death rates to advances in cardiovascular surgery (stents and so on) and chemotherapy, in addition to earlier diagnosis. This ignores the fact that people in the modern world are also becoming more obese; eating more fried foods, junk food and meat. So it is like taking a step forward along with a step back.

Our medical institutions are remarkable in their ability to artificially extend privileged patients' lives through intervention. In some cases, these heroic efforts may add a few quality years to a person's lifespan. In many cases, however, the intervention merely temporarily delays the inevitable. Unfortunately for many, those extended years are often spent drugged, incapacitated and sometimes even unconscious.

Cellular death

Every cell in the body has a programmed time to die. This genetic clock is subject to change according to our activities, however.

Cellular death is called apoptosis. This can be programmed death driven either by an internal clock. Or by means of an external condition that infects the cell.

Biologists have been investigating apoptosis' mysterious processes over the past few decades. Cell death can occur through a combination of several signaling circuits.

One involves a programmed shutdown of the mitochondria (the energy production facilities of the cell), seemingly associated with the production of a signaling biochemical called the cytochrome-c. This signaling follows the development of a special signaling channel called the MAC (mitochondria apoptosis channel).

The development of this special biocommunication channel appears mysterious. Still, we can surmise that this is simply part of the overall body's clockwork mechanism.

Scientists have also found that apoptosis also involves a complex process involving the internal self-destruct mechanism called tumor necrosis factor. The TNF mechanism was originally discovered in cancer research as the mechanism inhibiting the spread of a cancer.

Researchers have since found that its process is related to several other mechanisms. These include the R1 and R2 receptor mechanisms. The R1 and R2 receptors receive signals from outside the cell to stimulate a process of shutting down the cell. The TNF signaling process instigates a cascading communication process called *death-induced signaling*. Here one signal to the R1 or R2 receptors stimulates a multi-instructional process that begins shutting down the cell.

Part of this signaling process is transmitted through a genetic protein expression called the *p53 gene*. The p53 gene is a transcription protein affecting the process genetic copying. Researchers have discovered that many viruses and carcinogenic mutations are allowed to expand by disabling the p53 gene as well.

Another major signaling TNF mechanism is the *Fas-ligand* system. The Fas ligand is a specialized protein that signals to a receptor located on one of the chromosomes of the cell's DNA. This stimulation by the ligand—the signal-sending protein—seems to have its foundation in the T-cell immune system. As T-cells are activated, Fas ligands become more prolific, signaling the process of cell death.

In many circumstances, this also initiates a halting of the process of mitosis—causing cells to die without replacements. In situations where a cell is infected by a virus or a carcinogenic mutation, halting of mitosis signaling can be inhibited by viral DNA mutations.

By blocking the process of cell death, these viral mutations can multiply through cellular division. This allows the virus to replicate throughout the body.

The body's master instructional mechanisms maintain that subtle programming feature scientists refer to as homeostasis. Homeostasis in this context describes the body's ability to balance the number of cells that die with the number of new cells developed through cellular division or mitosis. This balancing act is a programming feature that is extremely complex.

Free radicals

These internal mechanisms of cellular death are often driven by external conditions. One of the most prominent is the input of free radicals.

Studies have investigated the body's biological clock—linked to DNA and the methylation of DNA—also referred to as epigenetic aging.

But a more tangible approach to aging and disease is the understanding that disease and the aging of the cell is linked to free radicals and oxidative stress. This is more tangible because we can chemically determine levels of oxidative stress in an individual.

In addition, research over the last few years has concluded that oxidative stress—damage to the body's tissues and cells from free radicals—increases with age.

But this has neither been confirmed nor quantified with regard to how much oxidative stress increases over the years.

Technology and recent research now affords scientists the ability to quantify the level of oxidative stress within an individual's body. And this quantification can be done at a particular period of time, with comparisons made.

In the first study of its kind, researchers from Italy's University of Bologna conducted a study of 247 healthy people who were between two days old and 104 years old. The researchers utilized a technique called electron paramagnetic resonance to test the blood of each of the people for their level of oxidative stress.

The test is similar to a nuclear magnetic resonance (NMR) but it also scans unstable measures molecules—considered oxidative and described as free radicals.

As expected, the researchers found that oxidative stress levels increase from childhood into the elderly years. But they also found that the rate of oxidative stress increases by an average of 1.1 percent per year. They also found there was little difference in this oxidative stress progression between men and women.

Some of the techniques and philosophy was born from a study that utilized electron paramagnetic resonance to study the oxidative stress levels of patients with sickle cell related thalassemia—a recessive blood disorder. The researchers tested 38 of the patients and compared their results with healthy control subjects that were matched—same age and so on.

The researchers found that the electron paramagnetic resonance results coincided with levels of oxidative stress determined from the blood of the patients.

They called the electron paramagnetic resonance testing a "radical probe."

The "radical probe" is referring to counts of free radicals, which are present in all of our bodies to one degree or another. Other research has found that free radical levels tend to be higher in disease—related to oxidative stress.

Free radicals are highly produced from toxins, but are generally produced from nature as well. Multiple studies over the years have shown that our synthetic chemical society has become more harmful in general because of the increases in free radicals produced by consuming these chemicals.

This doesn't mean that nature also produces free radicals. It does. Free radicals are a natural part of metabolism. As long as we don't get bombarded with them by consuming synthetic toxins.

What these researchers determined is that high levels of free radicals are proportionate to higher levels of oxidative stress because free radicals need electrons. As they steal electrons from cells and tissues, those remaining molecules will often combine one way or another with oxygen—producing an oxidation reaction.

And because such an free radical-caused oxidation reaction will in effect rip away molecules from tissues and cells, the result is disease and aging.

But now we know—from the University of Bologna study discussed above—that levels of free radicals increase over the years. We also know that they increase in a fairly uniform and predictable manner.

If we assume the rate of free radical intake is constant, this means the body is slowing down its ability to neutralize free radicals over time. This relates directly to the liver's production of glutathione, superoxide dismutase and others, as well as the ability of our immune system and probiotic system to neutralize free radicals as we age.

While this in itself does not explain how we age—because we don't know why these mechanisms are slowed down with aging—understanding this allows a new understanding of how we can reduce our proclivity to disease as we age.

This of course gives us a means to help slow the process of cell and tissue damage as we age—by decreasing our exposure to toxins as our bodies get older.

The Role of Antioxidants

The potential means for combating degenerative disease is to increase consumption of antioxidants.

Antioxidants are foods, nutrients and phytocompounds we can consume that will naturally neutralize free radicals. Even if our liver and immune system is slowing down as we age, we can increase our intake of antioxidants to help defer degenerative disease.

If we are increasing our antioxidant consumption by at least by 1% per year to keep up with our free radical increases, we stand a chance to seriously defer degenerative diseases, which include cancers, Alzheimer's and others.

This doesn't mean we can live forever in these bodies. Aging is part of nature's way of telling us this lifetime is only a part of our journey. But perhaps we can keep our body and mind a little healthier—and more useful—during this part.

Antioxidants and cancer

Research from scientists from Brussels has confirmed that skin cancer is related directly to oxidative stress—and other research shows antioxidants reduce oxidative stress.

The new research comes from the Brussels' Central Hospital, University of Charleroi, and the Hospital Vesale Experimental Medicine Laboratory at Free University of Brussels. The researchers tested 36 patients with head and neck squamous cell carcinomas—one of the most lethal forms of skin cancer. The researchers collected the tumor tissues of the 36 patients along with close-by tissue without tumors.

The researchers then conducted an in-depth analysis of the tissues and tested them using capillary electrophoresis—testing that separates and breaks down tissues into their smaller components. The researchers also conducted oxidation testing and specifically determined the ratios between oxidized glutathione and reduced glutathione.

The ratio of oxidized glutathione to reduced glutathione in the tissues relates directly to the amount of oxidative stress in the tissues, as well as indicates the level of antioxidant activity. This is because glutathione is the leading scavenger of oxidation within the body.

The researchers found that the tumor tissues showed significantly higher variation in the glutathione GSH part of the ratio. This indicates that the free scavenging abilities of glutathione are reduced within skin cancer tissue.

Nine out of ten cancers on the head and neck are squamous cell carcinomas. About half of those with this cancer will die within five years.

The Brussels research confirms findings from the University of Oslo in Norway. In this study, the researchers compared 78 patients with head and neck squamous cell carcinoma together with 100 healthy people.

This time the researchers tested the tissues and blood of all the participants for levels of oxidative stress related to not only glutathione, but also hydroperoxides, gamma-glutamyl transpeptidase, prostagladin and oxidized/total ascorbic acid levels.

The researchers also tested for levels of antioxidants present in all the subjects—including total antioxidant capacity, glutathione redox potential, total glutathione levels and total cysteine levels. They also tested all the subjects for dietary antioxidant levels—including six different carotenoids (carrots and tomatoes are high in carotenoids), four tocopherols (seeds, grains and oils are high in tocopherols, and ascorbic acid (fruits are high in ascorbic acid).

The researchers found that the patients with squamous cell carcinoma all had higher levels of oxidative stress biomarkers in their blood and tissues. The levels of total hydroperoxides were significantly higher in the skin cancer patients—indicating specifically that their bodies were under oxidative stress.

The researchers also found that these oxidative stress markers went up significantly when the cancer patients underwent radiation treatment.

The researchers also found that the skin cancer patients lower levels of the dietary antioxidants within their bloodstream as compared with the healthy control subjects. They also found that the levels of antioxidants fell dramatically as the patients were subjected to radiation treatment.

Okay, we get that: Antioxidants can help improve survival rates among patients with skin cancer, and help patients deal with radiation treatment. But how about preventing cancer altogether by eating a healthy diet with lots of antioxidants, and reducing those lifestyle habits—such as smoking and alcohol consumption—that have been specifically linked with producing higher levels of oxidative stress in the body?

Antioxidants are most prevalent in fruits and vegetables. This means consuming more fruits and vegetables will lengthen our lives and help delay our departure from the body. Eating more antioxidants will also decrease our risk of Alzheimer's disease and other forms of dementia.

There are also other dietary strategies to consider. I have covered these in detail in my book, "The Ancestors Diet." Specific strategies to help prevent or delay Alzheimer's disease can be found in my book, "Holistic Remedies for Alzheimer's Disease."

Fulfilling Life with Love

A fulfilling life comes in the form of love. How much love did we give others around us? How much love did we generate from our relationships, activities and accomplishments?

When we consider our coming departure from this world, how much love we left in the world is tantamount to our real impact upon the world.

Every day we find gracious acts that people do as an expression of their love for others. We find people saving the lives of others. We find people who encourage others. We find people who work tirelessly for the welfare of others. Such activities work to not just help others. But they also encourage others to help others.

In other words, love is infective.

These acts are sometimes small and unseen. But they are still infective, no matter how small. They are infective because they are fulfilling to our soul.

Should we seek to help others in the course of accomplishing our goals, we will also encourage others to care for others. In other words, we can spike our plan with love—which will infect others with love as well.

This is how we can coordinate our plan for life with love: And coordinate our hearts with God.

Getting our Affairs in Order

This is an expression that people will use when death appears to be impending. The expression assumes the person hasn't been keeping their affairs in order. As if there are things that the person has been procrastinating over and has yet to take care of.

Many will think this relates to life insurance. Yes, life insurance may well be important if we are supporting a family that would need help should we depart. For this we can have a talk with a trusted insurance agent.

But this phrase often refers to one's will or trust. If a person dies without leaving a will, then no one will know what to do with their things after they die.

The term for dying without a will is being *intestate*.

The intestate situation typically forces the legal system to follow protocols on where the assets go after death. Here is the typical priority for the legal system, in terms of where intestate assets go:

- The spouse (assuming community property)
- If there is no spouse, the children
- If no spouse or children, the parents or their children (siblings)
- If no parents or siblings, then to cousins.
- If no cousins, then to the state.

This is besides the probate taxes that will be charged on inheritance. Inheritance taxes have been changing over the years, with larger maximum exclusion levels. Depending upon the state or country and year of death, the inheritance tax may be as great as 46 percent of the estate after the exclusion. Over the past few years, this exclusion has been growing in the U.S., up to $5.45 million.

This can and has been changing. In 2001, it was only $675,000 in the U.S.

The bottom line is that if we do not have 'our affairs in order,' the state will determine where our estate ends up. And much of it, if not all of it, may end up belonging to the state in the form of taxes.

It's Not About the Money

Often people consider what a person leaves behind in money terms only. This is short-sighted.

This is not all about the money. It's about love. Relationships.

First, whatever money is left to someone in a will represents how the departed felt about the person. What is the message being sent?

Such a message typically refers to the relationship between the departed and those they are close to.

Whether a person inherits or doesn't inherit will typically go to the core of their relationship with the departed. The departed may have put up with the person while they were alive for one reason or another. But how they decided to direct their estate after the death of their body is a more true reflection about how they felt about the person.

That can be tough to take on the receiving or non-receiving end. A person who felt they had a nice relationship with the departed, only to find out the will directed the estate elsewhere can feel hurt and surprised.

For this reason, it is important for us to get this right. Our will or trust is a communication after we leave—to those who were around us when we were here.

If we depart without a will, the government will step in and determine who gets what. Our immediate family members will be our automatic heirs. But is this what we want? Will this communicate what we want to those who cared for us?

Or, if we leave with a will or trust that is not updated, which considers our current relationships, we may end up hurting people. Those who took care of us during our final years may feel stiffed if we don't even consider their love for us after we pass from the body.

Then of course, we can choose to donate all of our estate to charity, or to some particular purpose we had during our life. This is also a clear communication to those around us about what our life stood for.

In any case, we also need to consider our personal effects. Do we want our family members squabbling over who should have our personal or even valuable heirlooms? What about our jewelry? Our clothing? Our furniture? Our computers? How about books that we wrote or songs that we recorded? These may not seem valuable to us now. And it may seem trivial that we direct who should have them.

But again, this is a communication. By directing that a certain person or persons receive certain personal effects can mean the world to those persons. This may indeed be one of the most important communications we leave those who were around us before we left our body.

Of course, the communication can be love or disdain. It could be disappointment.

Or we could, as many have in the past, leave our estate and/or personal effects with certain requirements. We may want a child to graduate from college, for example, before they get a lump sum. So we install that requisite into our trust or will—that they will receive the inheritance only after they graduate.

This is one example, but there are many other possibilities. We can communicate our wishes to those around us after we have left our body in many other ways. This may not seem that impactful as we consider it now. But when we leave, those we have left behind will be greatly affected by whatever directions we give through our will or trust.

Will or Trust?

I've mentioned both together in the above discussion because we do have an option.

A will is the document most of us are familiar with. The will appoints an executor who will administer the will—and arrange the directions of our estate by the instruction of the will. The will can direct our funds wherever we want. However, the will typically also comes with a price, in the form of a greater tax burden.

What is a trust?

A trust is a structure that can own a person's assets and estate. The trust can be revocable or irrevocable. A revocable trust means that the person who created the trust (trustor) can eliminate the trust at any time and reclaim the assets back to the trustees or trustor.

An irrevocable trust cannot be revoked by the trustor. It is more of a separate entity legally.

Estate trusts for the purpose of passing on one's assets are typically revocable trusts. An irrevocable trust can also be used, but a revocable trust gives the trustor and the trustees broader powers over the assets during their lifetimes.

After the passing of the trustor, the trust lives on. The trustees—assuming they are alive, can continue to manage the trust as if nothing happened. Or they can dissolve the trust and transfer the assets as needed.

This is a good facility for a person to pass on their estate without dealing with probate. This is because the trustees can transfer the assets or give trust rights to new trustees directly.

The estate trust can also continue the projects or business of the person who passes. Assuming the trust is managed by trustees who want to carry on those projects.

A trust can contain any asset or operation that a person can own. Under the law, a trust can be set up to be an independent entity.

The downside to the trust is that it requires some administrative effort to set it up and maintain it. This can be mitigated by professionals. For example, there are professional trust lawyers online who can set up a trust for you.

Trust lawyers can also help administer the trust after you depart. If the trust is set up as a means to pass on our estate, a trusted attorney can be chosen to administer the trust after the departure of the trustor. In this case, the trust will need to set up a clause that appoints the attorney as the replacement trustee when the trustor departs.

For those who are married, the estate trust can be set up so that the husband and the wife are the sole trustees, and it is only if both of them dies that new trustees are appointed and manage the trust from there.

At that point, the new trustee will operate the trust in line with the trust's instructions after the passing of the trustor(s).

It is important to contact a trusted attorney if you want to put together a trust. This summary provides only some basic information, but may not be applicable in some states or countries.

Perhaps a Will is Easier?

A will might be easier to set up and manage. This is because it requires setting up a single document. Once the will is drawn out, you just sign it and keep the document in a safe place. Giving a copy to your attorney, CPA or investment advisor is also a good idea.

Safe places include safe deposit boxes or safety boxes where we might keep their property documents or statements. Be sure to keep a second copy somewhere else in case of emergency.

The will is very basic. It directs where or to whom one's assets should be directed after one's passing. It also names an *executor*. A person who is responsible for paying out funds to heirs and paying debts to creditors (which usually will have to be done first.)

The executor can be a friend or family member, but we must also remember that this can be a heavy responsibility for someone who might be already emotionally burdened by our passing. If our estate has the resources, it might be better to have a trusted lawyer, accountant, investment advisor or other trusted third party execute the will.

The raw will document can be readily obtained from an attorney or certified public accountant who can help us write it up.

For do-it-yourselfers, raw will forms can also be downloaded online. There are some reputable legal firms online that provide will forms that comply with the particular laws of our state and country. This is important because many states and countries have different probate laws, so the will should comply with our state and country of residency.

It is best to have the will notarized or at least witnessed by someone outside of one's immediate family. An attorney or notary public is good for such a case.

In this case, one should arrange with the attorney ahead of time and become clear on what the attorney will charge the estate for his/her services.

A qualified attorney can handle the entire matter of a will, and also let you know the advantages and disadvantages of a trust.

Be sure to ask about taxes. Wills generally are executed through probate, which exacts taxes depending upon the country and state of probate. These rates can also change, so once we already have a trust or will in place we might want to keep up with the news on estate tax rates.

The overriding message of death relates to more than putting our monetary affairs in order. It also means thinking through our legacy. How do we want to be remembered? How do we want to have affected others? What kind of contribution will we have made with our life?

Certainly, as Socrates told his students when they asked him how he wanted to be buried, we will be long gone by then. But legacy can include our estate maintaining our projects and goals after our departure. With some creativity, we can continue our legacy with respects to helping others. Spouses, friends and family are often willing to help continue our charitable projects.

Such a continuation requires something in writing or otherwise recorded. This allows us to clarify our goals and objectives in this regard.

The Need for Inventory

In the 2nd chapter we discussed the need for taking an inventory of our lives. This personal inventory covered our passions, strengths, weaknesses, working assets as well as liabilities. The focus here was upon our personal strengths and weaknesses.

In order to develop a good will or trust, we also need an inventory. But this inventory is focused upon a physical inventory of our physical assets and liabilities.

These sorts of assets and liabilities include stuff like real estate, bank accounts, insurance policies, 401Ks and/or IRA accounts. They also include personal effects like jewelry, cars, furniture, memorabilia and so forth.

Personal effects can easily be missed in this process. But those family and friends that we leave behind often put much greater value on our personal effects than we might. Why? Because these things will continue to remind our loved ones of us. They provide a means of connection to us long after we are gone.

Certainly, we might want to leave a significant amount of our physical assets like money to those we feel might need it the most. This can include charities or family members. But we should not forget others who offered us their love, kindness or even their time.

Such persons could receive from us, for example, a cherished painting or some other personal effect. Such things can communicate to them how much we have cared about them.

Communicating to those we leave behind when we leave this world can be a great source of healing as well. People will surely miss us when we are gone. Communicating to them through our will or trust is a special thing.

The Charitable Legacy

Charitable giving through our will or trust is a great way to cement our personal legacy, and our love for others. Giving to a cause that we have believed in and have been caring about during our life provides a facility to give our lives great meaning.

As we leave our bodies, this will give us great comfort. Leaving whatever remaining assets and our life savings to causes that care for others provides a respite from a world where many are looking out for themselves or their families. Should our families be in a comfortable position or otherwise able to manage without an inheritance—or have enough inheritance to do so—the rest can be given to charities.

Many of us might feel that we would like to help people in need but we may not have had enough resources to contribute what we would have liked to contribute during our lifetimes.

Our will or trust provides such a mechanism to contribute all or much of our assets to our favorite charities.

Clinical Death Research

As we discussed earlier, the reality proven out by science is that each of will live on after our body dies. This means we will continue to exist after the time of death comes. Thanks to scientific research, such a notion is not solely one of faith. It is now a matter of fact.

Evidence concluding we are distinct from the physical body has been presented by a number of respected medical researchers over the past five decades. With the advent of resuscitation and medical life-support technologies has come a proliferation of patients whose bodies have clinically died prior to resuscitation.

Author and researcher Dr. Raymond Moody pioneered this research in the 1960s, and introduced us to the *near death experience* (or NDE).

In his 1975 publication, Dr. Moody presented hundreds of cases documenting common experiences among patients declared clinically dead in a clinical setting. Dr. Moody's research reviewed a cross-section of thousands of cases of patients with a variety of religious and socio-economic backgrounds.

Dr. Moody and his associates discovered a common experience: After separating from the body, the person often floats above it, viewing the various resuscitation efforts taking place on the body.

This is often followed by the self remotely traveling to and viewing loved ones. Often traveling at the speed of thought to their homes or locations, the self tries in vain to communicate with their loved one(s).

Afterward, many subjects detailed being drawn into a darkened tunnel with a bright light at the end. At the end of the tunnel, many encountered a dazzling light and/or person. Many reviewed their lives in an instant. Some spoke with this personality. In some cases the personality indicated it was "not their time yet." Following this, they instantly returned to their body.

This usually coincided with the revival of the body, often while being resuscitated. While specific details of the experiences were different, nearly all NDE subjects experienced the separation from their physical body and felt at least peaceful.

Naturally, this research had its skeptics. A few questioned Dr. Moody's protocols such as patient selection and interview techniques. These gaps were quickly filled by Kenneth Ring, Ph.D. In a well-received peer-reviewed study published in 1985, Dr. Ring randomly selected 101 patients who had experienced an NDE.

Dr. Moody's patients were collected as their cases were presented to him. This offered some but not complete randomness. By contrast, the 101 patients studied by Dr. Ring were chosen randomly to eliminate any bias, imagination, hallucination, inconsistency, and other elements possibly affecting the objectivity of their after-death experiences.

Of the 101 subjects, a third reported out-of-body experiences, and a quarter reported entering the darkness or tunnel with the light at the end. About 60% reported at least a positive, peaceful experience. Those NDE subjects whose death was the result of a suicide attempt experienced no tunnel or light. The suicide NDEs in this study experienced a "murky darkness" after feeling separated from their body, but did not proceed any further. The rest had little or no recollection of the experience.

Dr. Ring's findings—though not in the exact same percentages—were substantiated by professor of medicine and cardiologist Michael Sabom, M.D. in a 1982 work called *Recollections of Death: A Medical Investigation*. There have been several other studies confirming NDE experiences as well.

In addition, Dr. Elisabeth Kubler-Ross documents researching some twenty thousand cases of near-death in her 1991 book *On Life After Death*, confirming the same primary conclusions of the early research done by Sabom, Moody and Ring.

Upon review of the other various explanations, it appears unlikely that any of the possible physical causes could suitably explain NDE. The only reasonable explanation is that the self is not the body. The sheer cross-section of people with this same experience provides too much variance to provide any other rational explanation.

The common NDE experiences in these cases occurred regardless of the level of religious reverence, expectation levels, drug-administration, knowledge of NDE and brain or biochemical stimulation.

Additionally, when both Moody and Sabom tested the observations of NDE out-of-body observations with hospital staff, they almost without exception confirmed the observations the NDE subjects made from outside of a body that was clinically unconscious.

While unconscious and with eyes closed, a patient could hardly be expected to observe such events—even if by subconscious hearing.

By far the most logical and scientific conclusion to the evidence—in addition to the evidence presented in the 3rd chapter—is that the self is truly a separate entity, and once the body dies, the self departs.

The Message of Dying

With these points in mind, we can conclude death as not an end, but a transition. The departure from a temporary vehicle, and a continuation of our unique journey.

Furthermore, this research indicates we will definitely be reflecting upon our lives after we leave our body. This means that now is the time to arrange our lives and our legacy in such a way as to minimize our regrets.

The dying of the body thus has a clear message: It is time for us to depart this phase in our journey. It is time for a new adventure. Our learning within this lifetime has come to an end and we are ready for a new journey. It is time for us to move on.

Death is like being shown the door. When we are visiting with friends at their house and our hosts suddenly get up off the sofa and begin to slowly walk towards the door, we know it is time to leave. It is time to move on, thank our host for the fun time, and say goodbye. It is not time to start up another conversation or go back and sit on the sofa. Should we do this, we will probably be accused of 'overstaying our welcome.'

True Life Extension

The natural body is simply not designed to live forever. Our western medical institutions tease us with notions of new technologies that can keep the body alive forever. We should know this will not be a reality, however. Nor is it a good use of our precious time while here.

The laws of nature have a reason. We inhabit a physical body for a short time to learn specific lessons. It is a short-term vehicle. The body is not meant to house the living being forever. It is like putting on a spacesuit with a particular oxygen reserve. Once within the temporary spacesuit, a smart astronaut does not waste time debating about why there is not more oxygen in the tank. It is what it is, and the astronaut has a particular job to do before returning to the space ship.

The problem is that we begin to falsely identify with the physical body after a few years in it. This is also by design. Once this misidentification grabs us—which happens pretty early on in our lives in this body—we become connected to our body. We try to protect it at all costs. We scream when it becomes threatened. We raise our hackles when a life-threatening challenge presents itself.

We have discussed how the body, mind and self can be deceived by a misinterpretation of stress as a potentially life-threatening event. Our body can be pumping out emergency biochemicals and waveforms even when little is at stake.

This misinterpretation can also be evident during a truly life-threatening situation. We have often seen situations where people become so anxious during a traumatic experience that they do not react appropriately. We might do the wrong thing under the circumstances. We might scream when in reality no one could hear us or help us. We might freeze like a deer in the headlights when we should be running from a threat.

During the 9/11 disaster some people reacted calmly and intelligently during the disaster and evacuated orderly while helping others, while a significant number of people panicked and did not act appropriately. Most of us agree that an over-stimulated panic state can sometimes be a distraction or even a deterrent from dealing with an emergency. For this reason, most of us consider a state of panic with disdain. We also give respect to those who coolly and calmly react during a crisis.

Why do we respect those who calmly react appropriately in a crisis? This is because most of us see a state of panic as being disconnected from the reality of an emergency. An overstated panic response is often seen in groups. A panicking group of people can easily over-react and over-step the boundaries of what should take place.

This is typically because these people are watching everyone else's response rather than assessing the situation directly. As a result, they are out of touch with the problem and tend to react as others do. Research has showed that in an emergency, crowds tend to immediately select a group leader or role model—often arbitrarily. As the inherited leaders of the group respond, the rest of the group is likely to respond similarly.

Should these 'chosen ones' react inappropriately, the entire crowd responds in kind. Suddenly the situation becomes a crisis because an entire group or population of people responded inappropriately to a perceived threat. We might call this the *herd mentality*.

This is precisely the situation existing today amongst our medical institutions with regard to the process of death.

It is appropriate to respond to a patient who has been shot or injured. Attempts are made to extract the bullet or repair the injury. These are acceptable responses to a critical injury that may easily be healed with intervention. Heroic attempts to resuscitate an individual who has had a heart attack or someone who has had a stroke would be considered appropriate as well.

There is a critical line, however, between these types of emergency interventions and unacceptable attempts to intervene in the natural process of death. The line between the two becomes evident when the body is chronically malfunctioning and pain without medication is unbearable.

As we have discussed previously, tens of thousands of near-death experiences have documented real experiences after the clinical death of the body. Most documented clinical death experiences include the self first floating up over the body and looking down upon it, and seeing the doctors and nurses operating or attempting resuscitation.

Thousands of these unembodied observations have been confirmed as accurate. This is physically impossible for a body lying in a bed unconscious.

Life Support

So we must now ask this important question: Knowing the body will inevitably become obsolete and we will separate from it, why should we respond inappropriately to the prospect of death?

Why should we unnaturally keep a person from the next step in their journey, and keep them in a state of suspension with artificial respiration and feeding tubes? There is little quality of life in living out a few months in a hospital bed attached to life-support equipment, unable to conduct meaningful physical or mental activities.

Certainly, doctors are encouraged to valiantly rescue a dying person. However, we all know examples of situations where heroic efforts become questionable. Most of us have heard of cases where a person is kept on resuscitating equipment well past a reasonable period of time. The patient remains unconscious, and without the equipment the body would surely cease existing.

During this time, the inner self is trapped within the body and not being let go. The self is stuck without the ability to communicate their preferences. What can we do?

Note that we are not making a determination here of where the line should be drawn, or isolating which types of resuscitation are reasonable. This is a personal decision that should be made by each of us. Each of us is responsible for the efforts that others make on behalf of our body's survival.

Therefore each of us is responsible for making the determination for the limitation of heroic efforts, and making this clear (in writing) to our relatives and health professionals.

In the absence of such a direction in writing, artificial life support will become the decision of our spouse or relatives.

This is a very difficult position to be in as a relative. Any caring spouse or family member will struggle with such a decision, because they do not want their mate or relative to leave them. Who would want to be responsible for letting their loved one go?

They also may be presented with the appearance of wanting to hasten the death of their spouse or family member. Putting our spouse or relatives in this position is simply unfair.

Sometimes, in the absence of clear instructions by the dying person, a court or legislative body will become involved in the decision of whether to disconnect the person from their life-support equipment. Why should we put others in this uncomfortable position? Why should we involve total strangers in the decision about whether we wish to be let go or not?

This is not to say that we should not work to keep our body in good condition as long as it is useful. Keeping the body in good condition will allow it to run efficiently and effectively.

However, once our bodies have played out their intended era, we can embrace death as a natural progression of our physical journey. Instead of struggling to survive at all costs, we can use our remaining time to consider the meaning of life. We can begin transcending the physical world and seek clarity on our spiritual existence.

This is the purpose of advanced age. We no longer need to be concerned about career advancement. There's no future retirement to consider. We can certainly remain active through our advanced years. A weakening of our physical abilities occurs for a reason. It is time to focus on and prepare for our transition.

Instead, our health care industry often works to distract those of advanced years from this mission. For this reason, pharmaceutical drug use is rampant among those of advanced age. Being distracted with mind-numbing drugs is not a good use of our remaining time. The importance of a clear mind to use for spiritual contemplation and reflection should not be downplayed.

Certainly, advanced in modern medicine have allowed us to extend our lifetimes. This is not necessarily a bad thing. We are now able to transplant hearts, install stents and replace kidneys.

The more important questions: Are these attempts to extend our physical life really extending the quality of our lives? Is there a net gain after we consider the time spent on the effort? Some transplants like kidneys might be reasonable. Others, like heart transplants, are risky and often only temporarily extend the inevitable.

How do we decide? We might use the same kind of logic we would use to decide whether to drive or fly to a destination. We would compare the driving and stopping times to the airport lines and waiting times, the flight, and the travel to and from the airport. Depending upon the distance, sometimes driving might be faster than flying. Or perhaps the flight is cheaper than the drive after gas and meals are considered.

The quality of our remaining life can be analyzed similarly. In measuring the cost of prolonging life, we have to net out how much time is taken by doctor's visits, hospitalization, surgery, recuperation, rehabilitation, various follow-up visits and of course the risks and side effects involved in treatment. This "process time" needs to be subtracted from the extra days or years gained from the treatment.

All of this time spent avoiding death should be subtracted from the net conscious time gained in order to assess the value of the treatment. This relates directly to the quality of life achieved. If the process leaves us unable to return to our families and lifestyle in a reasonable amount of time then what good was all the effort?

Included in this consideration is that much of the effort and expense for these doctors and hospitals could be spent on saving children who are dying of malaria, AIDS and other ailments. These children could well recover and have a significant quality of life remaining.

We should consider in this evaluation the many billions of dollars and time resources spent by many researchers, doctors, professionals, hospitals, pharmaceutical companies and insurance providers; all aimed at attempting to add a few days, months or a year or two to lives that have already lasted 70 or 80 years. Is it worth all this effort? What if all that effort went into preventing and treating congenital diseases in children, or other disorders in young people?

What if we were to put all of the money, energy and resources we spend trying to unnaturally stay alive towards caring for childhood sickness and feeding hungry people around the world?

We would probably live in a much kinder world, and be better prepared to leave it. We would probably also all live longer, as we would likely have less stress—a central cause of a majority of fatal diseases.

The bottom line is that a consciousness of kindness also makes our bodies healthier.

Currently the U.S. is number one in the world for per-capita spending on healthcare, yet ranked number fifty-eight for longevity. Much of our healthcare spending and resources is going to waste.

The United States' economy is drowning in medical costs. The current head of the Government Accounting Office admits that the cost of health care and pharmaceuticals in the United States will bankrupt Medicare and possibly the entire government within a decade or two. Most Americans know this situation from the rising cost of health care, but many do not realize that health care costs have risen from 4% of America's gross national product in 1950 to a whopping 18% in 2010.

Death by Institution

The research on the causes of this healthcare crisis reveals that the cost of new equipment and new pharmaceuticals are the leading causes. Increasingly new devices are being invented and manufactured. These are not only diagnostic tools, but also devices to artificially extend life. Many of these diagnostic tools are over-rated and sometimes not useful in the long run.

Much of the advances in technology have come in the form of life-extension equipment. Today ones body can easily become a surrogate of one of these machines long after the intended time of death has past. Furthermore, the cost of putting someone on these extravagant machines bankrupts thousands of Americans every year.

Meanwhile, newer pharmaceuticals have been developed that chemically extend life by artificially reducing inflammation, pain and nervous issues. These efforts are certainly commendable, and the intentions of some researchers may be valiant. Still, these efforts come with a considerable price, sometimes in the form of numerous side effects. New research has found that some of these medications increase the risk of dementia.

Interestingly, many of these new technologies and medicines create as many early deaths as they may temporarily prevent. Over the past few decades, our medical industry has become the leading cause of death and injury in the United States. Carolyn Dean, M.D., N.D., in her book *Death By Medicine* compiled the following statistics for 2005:

Hospital Adverse Reaction—106,000 Deaths
Medical Error—98,000 Deaths
Bedsores—115,000 Deaths
Infection—88,000 Deaths
Malnutrition—108,800 Deaths
Outpatient Adverse Reaction—199,000 Deaths
Unnecessary Procedures—37,136 Deaths
Surgery-Related—32,000 Deaths
Total Annual Deaths by Modern Medicine—783,936

This accounting of deaths out-numbers U.S. cardio-vascular disease death rates and cancer death rates. In 2002 for example, 450,637 people died of heart disease and about 476,009 died of cancer.

The *Journal of the American Medical Association* reported that in 1994, 2,216,000 Americans were either hospitalized, permanently disabled, or died as a result of pharmaceuticals.

The Nutrition Institute of America reported that over 20 million unnecessary antibiotic prescriptions are typically prescribed each year. Over seven million medical and surgical procedures a year are unnecessary. Over eight million people are hospitalized without need. Our medical institution is quite simply suffocating in its own mismanagement.

According to a nationwide poll conducted by Louis Harris and Associates released in 1997 by the National Patient Safety Foundation and the American Medical Association, an estimated 100 million Americans experienced a medical mistake: 42% of those randomly surveyed. Misdiagnosis and wrong treatments accounted for 40% of those mistakes. Medical medication errors accounted for 28% of these, and medical procedure errors accounted for 22% of these.

In a study of four Boston adult primary care practices involving 1202 outpatients, 27% (95% confidence) of responders experienced adverse drug events.

In a 2004 interview with Dr. Lucian Leape, an expert in patient safety and an author of a number of studies, reported that over the past ten years since the 1997 NPSF studies were performed, improvements in our medical system have been inadequate. Barriers to improvement cited physician denial, hospital environment, lack of leadership and little system review.

As we consider these startling facts, we should realize this means our medical institutions' supposed heroic endeavors for life extension may actually cost more lives than they save in the long run. Some of these heroic efforts may actually shorten more lives than they extend.

To add insult to injury, the dramatically rising cost of medical care in our society also means less access to medical care for preventive care and non-critical treatment. In real terms, this means poorer people or the uninsured receive less healthcare, while preventive healthcare receives little attention.

Our medical institutions' heroic effort to save lives may be backfiring. Why? Because pharmaceutical and medical technology companies are madly pursuing profits while medical doctors are over-prescribing pharmaceuticals and over-applying diagnostic procedures in an attempt to avoid malpractice suits.

The United States has one of the lowest life expectancies among the industrialized world, while leading the world in the application of the newest technologies and healthcare costs. Meanwhile we see people living very long lives in places like Okinawa and Tibet, where medical technology and advanced drugs are less available.

There have been many discussions about some of these traditional cultures. Many have focused on the specifics of their lifestyles in an attempt to find some magic *'fountain of youth.'* In reality, these people live longer lives because they are living their lives in tune with nature.

Most of us living in industrialized society are faced with stress, processed foods and toxic environments, all of which shorten life span. We have traded in our blue skies for asbestos ceiling tiles and our sun for fluorescent lights. We traded air for soot and food for sugar and preservatives.

There has been a major shift in the types of diseases modern man is faced with. Third world countries and traditional cultures are faced with death from infectious epidemics and birth deaths. Western society, however, is challenged by a myriad of autoimmune disorders, cancers, heart disease and nervous disorders.

As a result of modern medicine's advancements, our doctors feel like superheroes when they temporarily extend the life of a person's body. This is regardless of the quality of life remaining with the patient. The quality of life of an advanced-age person undergoing multiple operations, medications, life-support equipment and severe chronic pain is obviously limited. Reduced to painkillers, heart-lung machines and ventilators, doctors are replacing the dignity of advanced age with zombied surrogates.

We must state clearly: *Old age is not a disease.*

These heroic efforts to save lives by doctors are certainly valiant. However, many activities in private medicine

are motivated simply by profits. Pharmaceutical companies and healthcare organizations are generally multi-
billion dollar enterprises built upon a mission of profit.

Their stockholders, directors, and management are
thus focused upon making profitable decisions. Controlled research clearly indicates that herbal remedies are
safe and effective over the long run with fewer side effects
when dosed correctly and knowledgeably. But pharmaceutical giants nevertheless use their influence to dissuade
people from using nature's healing agencies. Yet they have
isolated and patented many active constituents from me-
dicinal plants.

Despite their usefulness in preventing and treating
many conditions, herbal medicine is simply not profitable
for the pharmaceutical giants. Herbs are plants—and
plants are living organisms. For the most part, plants cannot be patented.

If we consider that hundreds of thousands of people
die each year from medications, while very few if any die
of herbal supplement use, the numbers simply do not imply a safety issue with herbs. Yet because they cannot be
patented, they are not supported by the pharmaceutical
and healthcare corporations built upon profitability and
market dominance.

Again, Dr. Lazarou calculated that over 2.2 million
people in the U.S. either end up being hospitalized, permanently disabled, or fatally injured resulting from
pharmaceutical use every year. That is over 2.2 million
Americans annually with *reported* injuries from pharmaceuticals. The study, done at the University of Toronto, also
showed that approximately 106,000 people die each year

from taking *correctly prescribed* FDA-approved pharmaceuticals.

This does not include the number of deaths resulting by overdose or by addiction to these same drugs. The U.S. FDA was sent 258,000 adverse drug events in 1999. Harvard researcher and associate professor of medicine Dr. David Bates told the *Los Angeles Times* in 2001 *"…these numbers translate to 36 million adverse drug events per year"*.

The plausibility of this number is confirmed in another study published in the *Journal of the American Medical Association* in 1995 led by Dr. Bates. This revealed that over a sixth month period, 12% of 4031 adult hospital admissions had either a confirmed adverse drug event or a potentially adverse drug event. If we extrapolate this rate using the population of 300 million Americans, we would arrive at the 36 million Rappoport calculated.

We might compare these horrific figures to effects of herbal medication usage—both prescribed and self-medicated. According to the FDA, a total of 184 deaths and 2,621 adverse reactions resulted from consumer use of herbal supplements *over a five-year period*. Most of the deaths were associated with incorrect use of weight-loss formulas and subsequent cardiac events.

Still, this is an average of 37 annual herbal deaths, compared to 108,000 deaths among pharmaceuticals. And 524 adverse herbal reactions per year to possibly 36,000,000 adverse pharmaceutical reactions per year. For those who might think that these numbers reflect that pharmaceutical use is much greater than herbal use; herbal supplementation use in the U.S. ranged from 27% to 36% of the population during that period. This nets out to about one-third of the population, which is higher than the range for prescription pharmaceutical use judging by elderly prescription rates as examined below.

For thousands of years, traditional doctors and scientists have carefully studied and documented particular botanicals associated with particular ailments. One of the earliest written records of herbal medicine is the *Pen Ts'ao*, written some 4,500 years ago by a Chinese herbalist.

The *Pen Ts'ao* recorded 366 different plant medicines and their specific uses. Ayurvedic texts—some even older—also document the use of hundreds of botanicals, as do the documents and spoken knowledge of the Greeks, the Romans, the Polynesians, the New Zealand Mauris, the Aborigines, the North American Indians, the Indonesians, the Mayans, the Egyptians, the Arabs, and the Northern Europeans.

Herbal medications have thus been used safely by billions of people over thousands of years.

In comparison, a pharmaceutical drug might be approved based on a few studies of several hundred patients, often managed by researchers paid by the pharmaceutical company. This means we can compare billions of traditional users of herbs unconnected with their commercial value versus data on a few hundred users of a particular drug organized by someone being paid by the manufacturer.

Once a pharmaceutical company has designed a new drug, it can receive patent protection for that chemical combination, giving them twenty years of potential exclusivity for selling that drug, at least in the United States. This means a 20-year guarantee of profits as long as doctors prescribe that drug.

Drug research by doctors—many of whom are also medical school professors—is typically funded by the pharmaceutical manufacturers. There is thus a built-in incentive for a successful outcome. As the cardiovascular and anti-inflammatory drug lawsuits have proved over the past few years, pharmaceutical manufacturers are often slow to disclose information that might damage the sales of their drugs.

Even if a pharmaceutical results in an improved condition for a particular ailment, there are often dangerous side effects. Some of these can be worse than the original ailment. In addition, most medications stress the liver and kidneys in one respect or another—shortening the lifespan of these critical organs.

Some medications, like aminoglycoside antibiotics streptomycin, kanamycin, garamicin and others have been shown to cause kidney damage in as many as 15 percent of patients. Others, such as acetaminophen, carbamazepine, atenolol, cimetidine, phenylbutazone, acebutolol, piroxicam, mianserin, naproxen, sulindac, ranitidine, enflurane, halothane, valproic acid, phenobarbital, isoniazid and ketoconazole can cause acute dose-dependent liver damage.

This is because the liver and the kidneys work together to process most chemicals out of the body. Together these organs break down and excrete the chemical by-products of medications, resulting in their hopeful extraction from the body. With this chemical breakdown comes a number of dangerous residual chemical derivatives.

The P450 liver enzyme process moves chemicals through the extraction pathway. This enzyme is effective in most healthy bodies for a few chemicals at a time. Yet multiple drugs can overwhelm and deplete this pathway. With the P450 extraction pathway overloaded by various chemicals, additional drugs can damage the body in a greater way. For this reason, a higher number of liver en-zymes in a blood analysis is seen by doctors as a dangerous sign.

Sadly, multiple drug prescribing is commonplace among the elderly. In America, a large number of elderly persons (especially those who regularly see a doctor) are taking multiple medications. A 2004 Duke University study showed that 21% or 7 million Americans over the age of 65 take drugs classified as "dangerous."

The over-65 population is 15% of the overall popula-tion, and this group is taking one-third of all drug prescriptions. Study researchers added that the study actu-ally understated the problem, and that an elderly person taking at least ten to twelve prescription drugs is common.

What this translates to is an elderly population being drugged through their "golden years." Because doctors are prescribing multiple mood-altering drugs to this group of people, we are left with an aging population of drug-dependency. Suddenly drugs become necessary for sleep. Drugs become needed to eat. Drugs become needed to maintain composure. Drugs become needed to get through the day.

Why have those of advanced age become increasingly drug-dependent? Primarily because advanced age can ma-ke us more vulnerable as we begin to face physical failings and pending death. After a lifetime of physical activity and an assumption that life was going to last forever, we can become insecure in our later years.

Drug advertising aimed at the elderly will typically show elderly people enjoying life, laughing and being active. This creates the message that the drug will help make us happy. Advertisers increasingly imply that drugs will create fulfillment and quality of life during a time meant for contemplation and introspection.

At a time when a person needs to have clarity and purpose of mind, our medical institutions are drugging us and tempting us with unrealistic expectations. As we approach the crossroads of our physical journey—and begin our transition from this body to our next destination—we need to be prepared for the true healing event.

What is the true healing event of our lives? It is the learning of the take-away points from a lifetime of lessons stemming from the challenges, growth, pain, laughter, love, relationships, losses, gains and finally the knowledge as we contemplate leaving it all behind. We thus need to utilize our faculties with clarity as we navigate this important step in our experience.

In other words, we must preserve our awareness.

Advance Healthcare Directives

There are several strategies we can execute to accomplish this. The first thing to consider putting in place is an advance healthcare directive. This can detail our wishes for how our body is medically cared for if we are no longer able to communicate those decisions directly.

The healthcare directive can therefore contain detailed instructions on health care activities we would consider acceptable with regard to critical care and ambulatory resuscitation. For example, the healthcare directive may instruct whether life support equipment is to be connected in the event we become unconscious.

It may also detail specific instructions, such as whether feeding tubes, blood transfusions, the heart-lung machine, ventilators, transplants and other care is acceptable to us, and if so, to what extent or for how long.

The healthcare directive can also be specific as to what types of medications are acceptable to us, and if so, how long those medications should be sustained. The healthcare directive can also specify other wishes regarding our medical care with the greatest of clarity and detail.

The health care advocate

A critical part of the healthcare directive is the appointment of a health care advocate. The health care advocate is a person we trust to oversee our health care treatment should we become hospitalized or incapacitated.

This person is also given the ability to make decisions on our behalf. Therefore, this person needs to be someone we trust implicitly to carry out our instructions as they are recorded in our healthcare directive.

In such a situation where we are deemed unable to make our own decisions, these instructions must be followed. It is important that our health care advocate have a copy of our healthcare directives so that he or she can show it to doctors and hospital administrators in the case of a our need for emergency treatment.

Many experts agree that without advance medical directives, we could be given medications we cannot or do not want to physically, mentally, emotionally or spiritually tolerate for long periods of time.

We may be given treatments that leave our bodies alive in suspended animation long after the body's intended death. Our bodies may end up being indefinitely hooked to life support equipment without our consent. In a suspended state, we may not be able to communicate our wishes to be let go.

Frequently this issue stresses families, doctors and hospital administrators as they debate the costs and treatment of a *coma, permanent vegetative state* (PVS), or *minimally conscious state* (MCS).

Comas will often be temporary, from a few hours to days, weeks or months. The vegetative and minimally conscious states are typically permanent, however. Many MCS and PVS cases evolve from coma states. MCS is accompanied by cognitive ability, while PVS and the coma state leave observers with a question of whether the person is even there. MRI brain scans have illustrated that MCS patients can both recognize speech and respond—if not physically, through their brainwaves.

Most coma and PVS patients appear to not be aware of their surroundings at all. The difference between a comatose and a PVS patient is simply that the PVS subject appears to be awake. This is deceptive, however, because there is still no apparent awareness in the PVS patient. All three states require life support systems—at least feeding tubes. MCS and PVS may only require a feeding tube, while PVS and coma states may also require ventilators.

People do wake up from comas, true. Yet waking up from PVS and MCS is rare. For this reason, the question of whether to maintain life through artificial means is quite controversial. Since the U.S. court system does not recognize coma, PVS or MCS as death, in the absence of specific instructions by the patient or their legal guardian, the hospital may keep these patients alive indefinitely. It is an ethical question that brings into focus the issue of what is death, and at what point should we let nature take its course?

Note that *euthanasia* or *mercy killing* is not being proposed here. Nor are we condoning suicide in any form, even its slower versions—namely alcoholism and drug abuse. Each of us has a designated time of death according to our consciousness and past behavior. No one has the right to interfere with our destiny. And if we interfere with our destiny, we will also be preventing lessons that we need to learn. If we don't learn those lessons now, we will have to learn them later.

Suicide or euthanasia is fooling around with our most precious asset—time. Time in itself may not seem precious, but it represents the ability to learn. Every moment we dwell within these bodies is accompanied by learning experiences. Even the event of death itself—our leaving the body—is a part of our learning experience.

At the same time, extending our body's life beyond its natural end is also fooling around with time. Yet each of us can make our own decision as to the meaning of "natural."

Each of us can and should make a personal decision of whether we want life support and if so, how long we want to be kept alive with life support should we become comatose, minimally conscious or vegetative. We can decide for ourselves how long medication will be given if any, and if so, what types of medication types are to be given.

We can also predetermine how much pain medication to be given as well. As we have discussed, pain is the body's signaling process that helps escort the inner self out of the body at the intended time. Opioids may have their place during the healing of painful events. They can also block pain from doing its intended job—possibly keeping our bodies struggling with an affliction long after nature intended. But they are also seriously addictive.

We can make our personal choices known with regard to coma, MCS or PVS in our healthcare directives. We can also have a clear conversation with our health advocate on how to oversee our decisions in case of our injury. The health advocate should be easily reachable in the case of our trauma or accident. Our nearest relative is suggested, but we might also consider that this nearest relative might have some conflict of interest in terms of letting go.

A close-by attorney could also be appropriate. Our advocate would approve medications being prescribed according to our wishes. They also can check to make sure those medications match the prescriptions written by the attending physician to avoid hospital errors. Many drug mistakes are made by attendants who misread the doctor's script or mistake one medication for another. The doctor may also not realize a medication allergy exists, and the advocate can clarify this.

The advocate can also monitor whether we are receiving enough fluids and are receiving a good diet during our stay in a hospital or home. Hospitals are notorious for serving overly processed and overly sweetened foods, which can spike our blood sugar and cause a variety of metabolic problems.

The advocate may request a special diet for us (hopefully plant-based foods with lots of fiber). They may also consider bringing bottled water, natural foods and supplements to us during their visits to the hospital. The doctor should be made aware of these, however.

Life-support systems may prove valuable in cases where a healthy body has been shot or involved in an accident. However, life-support systems used in enduring efforts to keep elderly people in their bodies past their appointed departure times could very well be classified as cruel and unusual punishment.

When it is our time to leave the body, we need to be let go. Natural efforts to restart the heart using the palms or opening the esophagus with the *Heimlich maneuver* may be appropriate. However, the endeavor to put the body on a heart and lung machine or other such invasive methods for a significant duration can enslave the inner self to a dysfunctional body without consciousness.

Planning for life also means planning for a departure that captures the essence of our life. Departing with a clear state of mind and a spiritual direction will give our life its crowning achievement. An achievement that allows us to embrace the life to come with wisdom and love in our hearts.

References and Bibliography

Ackerman D. A Natural History of the Senses. New York: Vintage, 1991.

Albrechtsen O. The influence of small atmospheric ions on human well-being and mental performance. Intern. J. of Biometeorology. 1978;22(4): 249-262.

Alexandre P, Darmanyan D, Yushen G, Jenks W, Burel L, Eloy D, Jardon P. Quenching of Singlet Oxygen by Oxygen- and Sulfur-Centered Radicals: Evidence for Energy Transfer to Peroxyl Radicals in Solution. J. Am. Chem. Soc., 120 (2), 396 -403, 1998.

Aronne LJ, Thornton-Jones ZD. New targets for obesity pharmacotherapy. Clin Pharmacol Ther. 2007 May;81(5):748-52.

Asimov I. The Chemicals of Life. New York: Signet, 1954.

Askeland D. The Science and Engineering of Materials. Boston: PWS, 1994.

Atkinson WW. Mind and Body: Mental States and Physical Conditions. LN Fowller/Progress Co. 1910.

Atkinson WW. Thought-Culture of Practical Mental Training. LN Fowller/Progress Co., 1909.

Atkinson WW. Vibration or the Law of Attraction in the Thought World. LN Fowler, 1906

Avanzini G, Lopez L, Koelsch S, Majno M. The Neurosciences and Music II: From Perception to Performance. Annals of the New York Academy of Sciences. 2006 Mar;1060.

Bache C. Lifecycles: Reincarnation and the Web of Life. New York: Paragon House, 1994.

Bachmann KA, Sullivan TJ, Jauregui L, Reese J, Miller K, Levine L. Drug interactions of H2-receptor antagonists. Scand J Gastroenterol Suppl. 1994;206:14-9.

Backster C. Primary Perception: Biocommunication with Plants, Living Foods, and Human Cells. Anza, CA: White Rose Millennium Press, 2003.

Baker SM. Detoxification and Healing. Chicago: Contemporary Books, 2004.

Ballentine R. Diet & Nutrition: A holistic approach. Honesdale, PA: Himalayan Int., 1978.

Ballentine RM. Radical Healing. New York: Harmony Books, 1999.

Bannerjee H. Americans Who Have Been Reincarnated. New York: Macmillan, 1980.

Barber CF. The use of music and colour theory as a behaviour modifier. Br J Nurs. 1999 Apr 8-21;8(7):443-8.

Barker A. Scientific Method in Ptolemy's Harmonics. Cambridge: Cambridge University Press, 2000.

Bates DW, Cullen DJ, Laird N, Petersen LA, Small SD, Servi D, Laffel G, Sweitzer BJ, Shea BF, Hallisey R, et al. Incidence of adverse drug events and potential adverse drug events. Implications for prevention. ADE Prevention Study Group. JAMA. 1995 Jul 5;274(1):29-34.

Batmangheilidj F. Neurotransmitter histamine: an alternative view point, Science in Medicine Simplified. Falls Church, VA: Foundation for the Simple in Medicine, 1990.

Batmangheilidj F. Your Body's Many Cries for Water. 2nd Ed. Vienna, VA: Global Health, 1992-1997.

Becker R. Cross Currents. Los Angeles: Jeremy P. Tarcher, 1990.

Becker R. The Body Electric. New York: William Morrow, 1985.

Beckerman H, Becher J, Lankhorst GJ. The effectiveness of vibratory stimulation in anejaculatory men with spinal cord injury. Paraplegia. 1993 Nov;31(11):689-99.

Bell IR, Baldwin CM, Schwartz GE, Illness from low levels of environmental chemicals: relevance to chronic fatigue syndrome and fibromyalgia. Am J Med. 1998;105 (suppl 3A).:74-82. S.

Beloff J. Parapsychology and radical dualism. J Rel & Psych Res. 1985;8, 3-10.

Benor D. Healing Research. Volume 1. Munich, Germany: Helix Verlag, 1992.

Bensky D, Gable A, Kaptchuk T (transl.). Chinese Herbal Medicine Materia Medica. Seattle: Eastland Press, 1986.

Bentley E. Awareness: Biorhythms, Sleep and Dreaming. London: Routledge, 2000

Berg A, Konig D, Deibert P, Grathwohl D, Berg A, Baumstark MW, Franz IW. Effect of an oat bran enriched diet on the atherogenic lipid profile in patients with an increased coronary heart disease risk. A controlled randomized lifestyle intervention study. Ann Nutr Metab. 2003;47(6):306-11.

Bergner P. The Healing Power of Garlic. Prima Publishing, Rocklin CA 1996.

Berman S, Fein G, Jewett D, Ashford F. Luminance-controlled pupil size affects Landolt C task performance. J Illumin Engng Soc. 1993;22:150-165.

Berman S, Jewett D, Fein G, Saika G, Ashford F. Photopic luminance does not always predict perceived room brightness. Light Resch and Techn. 1990;22:37-41.

Bernardi D, Dini FL, Azzarelli A, Giaconi A, Volterrani C, Lunardi M. Sudden cardiac death rate in an area characterized by high incidence of coronary artery disease and low hardness of drinking water. Angiology. 1995;46:145-149.

Bertin G. Spiral Structure in Galaxies: A Density Wave Theory. Cambridge: MIT Press, 1996.

Bishop B. Pain: its physiology and rationale for management. Part III. Consequences of current concepts of pain mechanisms related to pain management. Phys Ther. 1980 Jan;60(1):24-37.

Bitbol M, Luisi PL. Autopoiesis with or without cognition: defining life at its edge. J R Soc Interface. 2004 Nov 22;1(1):99-107.

Blackmore SJ. Near-death experiences. J R Soc Med. 1996 Feb;89(2):73-6.

Bockemühl, J. Towards a Phenomenology of the Etheric World. New York: Anthroposophical Press, 1985.

Boivin DB, Czeisler CA. Resetting of circadian melatonin and cortisol rhythms in humans by ordinary room light. Neuroreport. 1998 Mar 30;9(5):779-82.

Boivin DB, Duffy JF, Kronauer RE, Czeisler CA. Dose-response relationships for resetting of human circadian clock by light. Nature. 1996 Feb 8;379(6565):540-2.

Borchers AT, Hackman RM, Keen CL, Stern JS, Gershwin ME. Complementary medicine: a review of immunomodulatory effects of Chinese herbal medicines. Am J Clin Nutr. 1997 Dec;66(6):1303-12.

Borets VM, Lis MA, Pyrochkin VM, Kishkovich VP, Butkevich ND. Therapeutic efficacy of pantothenic acid preparations in ischemic heart disease patients. Vopr Pitan. 1987 Mar-Apr;(2):15-7.

Bose J. Response in the Living and Non-Living. New York: Longmans, Green & Co., 1902.

Bottorff JL. The use and meaning of touch in caring for patients with cancer. Oncol Nurs Forum. 1993 Nov-Dec;20(10):1531-8.

Bourgine P, Stewart J. Autopoiesis and cognition. Artif Life. 2004 Summer;10(3):327-45.

Braude S. First Person Plural: Multiple Personality and the Philosophy of Mind. Landham, MD: Rowman & Littlefield, 1995.

Brighenti F, Valtueña S, Pellegrini N, Ardigò D, Del Rio D, Salvatore S, Piatti P, Serafini M, Zavaroni I. Total Antioxidant Capacity of the Diet Is Inversely and Independently Related to Plasma Concentration of High-Sensitivity C-Reactive Protein in Adult Italian Subjects. Br J Nutr. 2005;93(5):619-25.

Britton WB, Bootzin RR. Near-death experiences and the temporal lobe. Psychol Sci. 2004 Apr;15(4):254-8.

Brodeur P. Currents of Death. New York: Simon and Schuster, 1989.

Brown V. The Amateur Naturalists Handbook. Englewood Cliffs, NJ: Prentice-Hall, 1980.

Brown, F. The rhythmic nature of animals and plants. Cycles. 1960 Apr:81-92.

Brown, J. Stimulation-produced analgesia: acupuncture, TENS and alternative techniques. Anaesthesia &intensive care medicine. 2005 Feb;6(2):45-47.

Browne J. Developmental Care—Considerations for Touch and Massage in the Neonatal Intensive Care Unit. Neonatatal Network. 2000 Feb;19(1).

Buck L, Axel R. A novel multigene family may encode odorant receptors: A molecule basis for odor recognition. Cell. 1991;65(April 5):175-187.

Buijs RM, Scheer FA, Kreier F, Yi C, Bos N, Goncharuk VD, Kalsbeek A. Organization of circadian functions: interaction with the body. Prog Brain Res. 2006;153:341-60.

Bulsing PJ, Smeets MA, van den Hout MA. Positive Implicit Attitudes toward Odor Words. Chem Senses. 2007 May 7.

Burr H, Lane C, Nims L. A Vacuum Tube Microvoltmeter for the Measurement of Bioelectric Phenomena. Yale Journal of Biology & Medicine. 1936;10:65-76.

Burr H. The Fields of Life. New York: Ballantine, 1972.

Buzsaki G. Theta rhythm of navigation: link between path integration and landmark navigation, episodic and semantic memory. Hippocampus. 2005;15(7):827-40.

Byrne R. The Secret. Beyond Words, 2006.

Cajochen C, Zeitzer JM, Czeisler CA, Dijk DJ. Dose-response relationship for light intensity and ocular and electroencephalographic correlates of human alertness. Behav Brain Res. 2000 Oct;115(1):75-83.

Calvin W. The Handbook of Brain Theory and Neural Networks. Boston: MIT Press, 1995.

Capitani D, Yethiraj A, Burnell EE. Memory effects across surfactant mesophases. Langmuir. 2007 Mar 13;23(6):3036-48.

Carroll D. The Complete Book of Natural Medicines. New York: Summit, 1980.

Cassileth B, Trevisan C, Gubili J. Complementary therapies for cancer pain. Curr Pain Headache Rep. 2007 Aug;11(4):265-9.

Chaitow L, Trenev N. ProBiotics. New York: Thorsons, 1990.

Chaitow L. Conquer Pain the Natural Way. San Francisco: Chronicle Books, 2002.

Cham, B. Solasodine glycosides as anti-cancer agents: Pre-clinical and Clinical studies. Asia Pac J Pharmac. 1994;9: 113-118.

Chaney M, Ross M. Nutrition. New York: Houghton Mifflin, 1971.

Chao A, Thun MJ, Connell CJ, McCullough ML, Jacobs EJ, Flanders WD, Rodriguez C, Sinha R, Calle EE. Meat Consumption and Risk of Colorectal Cancer. JAMA. 2005 January 12: 172-182.

Characterization and quantitation of Antioxidant Constituents of Sweet Pepper (Capsicum annuum—Cayenne). J Agric Food Chem. 2004 Jun 16;52(12):3861-9.

Chen-Goodspeed M, Cheng Chi Lee. Tumor suppression and circadian function. J Biol Rhythms. 2007 Aug;22(4):291-8.

Chilton F, Tucker L. Win the War Within. New York: Rodale, 2006.

REFERENCES AND BIBLIOGRAPHY

Chirkova E. Mathematical methods of detection of biological and heliogeophysical rhythms in the light of developments in modern heliobiology: A platform for discussion. Cybernet Sys. 2000;31(6):903-918.

Chong NW, Codd V, Chan D, Samani NJ. Circadian clock genes cause activation of the human PAI-1 gene promoter with 4G/5G allelic preference. FEBS Lett. 2006 Aug 7;580(18):4469-72.

Cocilovo A. Colored light therapy: overview of its history, theory, recent developments and clinical applications combined with acupuncture. Am J Acupunct. 1999;27(1-2):71-83.

Cohen S, Popp F. Biophoton emission of the human body. J Photochem & Photobio. 1997;B 40:187-189.

Cohen S, Popp F. Low-level luminescence of the human skin. Skin Res Tech. 1997;3:177-180.

Coles JA, Yamane S. Effects of adapting lights on the time course of the receptor potential of the anuran retinal rod. J Physiol. 1975 May;247(1):189-207.

Coll AP, Farooqi IS, O'Rahilly S. The hormonal control of food intake. Cell. 2007 Apr 20;129(2):251-62.

Conely J. Music and the Military. Air University Review. 1972 Mar-Ap.

Contreras D, Steriade M. Cellular basis of EEG slow rhythms: a study of dynamic corticothalamic relationships. J Neurosci. 1995 Jan;15(1 Pt 2):604-22.

Cook J, The Therapeutic Use of Music. Nursing Forum. 1981;20:3: 253-66.

Corkin S, Amaral DG, González RG, et al: H. M.'s medial temporal lobe lesion: findings from magnetic resonance imaging. J Neurosci. 1997;17:3964-3979.

Covey SR. The 7 Habits of Highly Effective People. Free Press, 1989.

Crawley J. The Biorhythm Book. Boston: Journey Editions, 1996.

Cruccu G, Aziz TZ, Garcia-Larrea L, Hansson P, Jensen TS, Lefaucheur JP, Simpson BA, Taylor RS. EFNS guidelines on neurostimulation therapy for neuropathic pain. Eur J Neurol. 2007 Sep;14(9):952-70.

Cummings M. Human Heredity: Principles and Issues. St. Paul, MN: West, 1988.

Curtis LH, Østbye T, Sendersky V, Hutchison S, Dans PE, Wright A, Woosley RL, Schulman KA. Inappropriate prescribing for elderly Americans in a large outpatient population. Arch Intern Med. 2004 Aug 9-23;164(15):1621-5.

Darrow K. The Renaissance of Physics. New York: Macmillan, 1936.

DaVinci L. (Dickens E. ed.) The Da Vinci Notebooks. London: Profile, 2005.

Davis GE Jr, Lowell WE. The Sun determines human longevity: teratogenic effects of chaotic solar radiation. Med Hypotheses. 2004;63(4):574-81.

Dawkins R. Climbing Mount Improbable. New York: Viking Press, 1996.

Dawkins R. The Selfish Gene. Oxford: Oxford UP, 1977 (1989 edition).

Dean C. Death by Modern Medicine. Belleville, ON: Matrix Verite-Media, 2005.

Dean E, Mihalasky J, Ostrander S, Schroeder L. Executive ESP. Englewood Cliffs, NJ: Prentice-Hall, 1974.

Dean E. Infrared measurements of healer-treated water. In: Roll W, Beloff J, White R (Eds.): Research in parapsychology 1982. Metuchen, NJ: Scarecrow Press, 1983:100-101.

Defrin R, Ohry A, Blumen N, Urca G. Sensory determinants of thermal pain. Brain. 2002 Mar;125(Pt 3):501-10.

Deitel M. Applications of electrical pacing in the body. Obes Surg. 2004 Sep;14 Suppl 1:S3-8.

Del Giudice E, Preparata G, Vitiello G. Water as a free electric dipole laser. Phys Rev Lett. 1988;61:1085-1088.

Delcomyn F. Foundations of Neurobiology. New York: W.H. Freeman and Co., 1998.

Dennett D. Brainstorms: Philosophical Essays on Mind & Psychology. Cambridge: MIT Press., 1980.

Dennett D. Consciousness Explained. London: Little, Brown and Co., 1991.

Depue BE, Banich MT, Curran T. Suppression of emotional and nonemotional content in memory: effects of repetition on cognitive control. Psychol Sci. 2006 May;17(5):441-7.

Dere E, Kart-Teke E, Huston JP, De Souza Silva MA. The case for episodic memory in animals. Neurosci Biobehav Rev. 2006;30(8):1206-24.

Devaraj TL. Speaking of Ayurvedic Remedies for Common Diseases. New Delhi: Sterling, 1985.

Devulder J, Crombez E, Mortier E. Central pain: an overview. Acta Neurol Belg. 2002 Sep;102(3):97-103.

Dhond RP, Kettner N, Napadow V. Neuroimaging acupuncture effects in the human brain. J Altern Complement Med. 2007 Jul-Aug;13(6):603-16.

Dolcos F, LaBar KS, Cabeza R. Interaction between the amygdala and the medial temporal lobe memory system predicts better memory for emotional events. Neuron. 2004 Jun 10;42(5):855-63.

Duke J. The Green Pharmacy. New York: St. Martins, 1997.

Duke M. Acupuncture. New York: Pyramid, 1973.

Dunne B, Jahn R, Nelson R. Precognitive Remote Perception. Princeton Engineering Anomalies Res Lab Rep. Princeton. 1983 Aug.

Ebbesen F, Agati G, Pratesi R. Phototherapy with turquoise versus blue light. Arch Dis Child Fetal Neonatal Ed. 2003 Sep;88(5):F430-1.

Eden D, Feinstein D. Energy Medicine. New York: Penguin Putnam, 1998.

173

Edris AE. Pharmaceutical and therapeutic potentials of essential oils and their individual volatile constituents: a review. Phytother Res. 2007 Apr;21(4):308-23.

Edwards B. Drawing on the Right Side of the Brain. Los Angeles, CA: Tarcher, 1979.

Edwards R, Ibison M, Jessel-Kenyon J, Taylor R. Light emission from the human body. Comple Med Res. 1989;3(2): 16-19.

Edwards R, Ibison M, Jessel-Kenyon J, Taylor R. Measurements of human bioluminescence. Acup Elect Res, Intl Jnl, 1990;15: 85-94.

Edwards, L. The Vortex of Life, Nature's Patterns in Space and Time. Floris Press, 1993.

Egon G, Chartier-Kastler E, Denys P, Ruffion A. Spinal cord injury patient and Brindley neurostimulation. Prog Urol. 2007 May;17(3):535-9.

Electromagnetic fields: the biological evidence. Science. 1990;249: 1378-1381.

Electronic Evidence of Auras, Chakras in UCLA Study. Brain/Mind Bulletin. 1978;3:9 Mar 20.

Elwood PC. Epidemiology and trace elements. Clin Endocrinol Metab. 1985 Aug;14(3):617-28.

Erdelyi R. MHD waves and oscillations in the solar plasma. Introduction. Philos Transact A Math Phys Eng Sci. 2006 Feb 15;364(1839):289-96.

Esch T, Stefano GB. The Neurobiology of Love. Neuro Endocrinol Lett. 2005 Jun;26(3):175-92.

Eschenhagen T, Zimmermann WH. Engineering myocardial tissue. Circ Res. 2005 Dec 9;97(12):1220-31.

Evans P, Forte D, Jacobs C, Fredhoi C, Aitchison E, Hucklebridge F, Clow A. Cortisol secretory activity in older people in relation to positive and negative well-being. Psychoneuroendocrinology. 2007 Aug 7

Exley C. Aluminium and iron, but neither copper nor zinc, are key to the precipitation of beta-sheets of Abeta in senile plaque cores in Alzheimer's disease. J Alzheimers Dis. 2006 Nov;10(2-3):173-7.

Falcon CT. Happiness and Personal Problems. Lafayette, LA: Sensible Psychology, 1992.

Filosa A, Valgimigli L, Pedulli GF, Sapone A, Maggio A, Renda D, Scazzone C, Malizia R, Pitrolo L, Lo Pinto C, Borsellino Z, Cuccia L, Capra M, Canistro D, Broccoli M, Soleti A, Paolini M. Quantitative evaluation of oxidative stress status on peripheral blood in beta-thalassaemic patients by means of electron paramagnetic resonance spectroscopy. Br J Haematol. 2005 Oct;131(1):135-40.

Flandrin, J, Montanari M(eds.). Food: A Culinary History from Antiquity to the Present. New York: Penguin Books, 1999.

Forget-Dubois N, Boivin M, Dionne G, Pierce T, Tremblay RE, Perusse D. A longitudinal twin study of the genetic and environmental etiology of maternal hostile-reactive behavior during infancy and toddlerhood. Infant Behav Dev. 2007 Aug;30(3):453-65.

Freeman W. The Physiology of Perception. Sci. Am. 1991 Feb.

Frey A. Electromagnetic field interactions with biological systems. FASEB Jnl. 1993;7: 272-28.

Fuster JM. Prefrontal neurons in networks of executive memory. Brain Res Bull. 2000 Jul 15;52(5):331-6.

Gabriel S, Schaffner S, Nguyen H, Moore J, Roy J. The structure of haplotype blocks in the human genome. Science. 2002;296:2225-2229.

Galaev, YM. The Measuring of Ether-Drift Velocity and Kinematic Ether Viscosity within Optical Wave Bands. Spacetime & Substance. 2002;3(5): 207-224.

Gambini JP, Velluti RA, Pedemonte M. Hippocampal theta rhythm synchronizes visual neurons in sleep and waking. Brain Res. 2002 Feb 1;926(1-2):137-41.

Gandhi T, Weingart S, Borus J, Seger A, Peterson J, Burdick E, Seger D, Shu K, Federico F, Leape L, Bates D. Adverse drug events in ambulatory care. N Engl J Med. 2003 Apr 17;348(16):1556-64.

Garcia-Lazaro JA, Ahmed B, Schnupp JW. Tuning to natural stimulus dynamics in primary auditory cortex. Curr Biol. 2006 Feb 7;16(3):264-71.

Gardner CD, Fortmann SP, Krauss RM. Association of small low-density lipoprotein particles with the incidence of coronary artery disease in men and women. JAMA. 1996 Sep 18;276(11):875-81.

Gau SS, Soong WT, Merikangas KR. Correlates of sleep-wake patterns among children and young adolescents in Taiwan. Sleep. 2004 May 1;27(3):512-9.

Gehr P, Im Hof V, Geiser M, Schurch S. The mucociliary system of the lung—role of surfactants. Schweiz Med Wochenschr. 2000 May 13;130(19):691-8.

Gerber R. Vibrational Healing. Sante Fe: Bear, 1988.

Ghayur MN, Gilani AH. Ginger lowers blood pressure through blockade of voltage-dependent calcium Channels acting as a cardiotonic pump activator in mice, rabbit and dogs. J Cardiovasc Pharmacol. 2005 Jan;45(1):74-80.

Glover J. The Philosophy of Mind. Oxford University Press, 1976.

Glück U, Gebbers J. Ingested probiotics reduce nasal colonization with pathogenic bacteria (Staphylococcus aureus, Streptococcus pneumoniae, and b-hemolytic streptococci. Am J. Clin. Nutr. 2003;77:517-520.

Gohil K, Packer L. Bioflavonoid-Rich Botanical Extracts Show Antioxidant and Gene Regulatory Activity. Ann N Y Acad Sci. 2002:957:70-7.

Goldberg B. Past Lives, Future Lives. New York: Ballantine, 1982.

REFERENCES AND BIBLIOGRAPHY

Golub E. The Limits of Medicine. New York: Times Books, 1994.

Gomes A, Fernandes E, Lima JL. Fluorescence probes used for detection of reactive oxygen species. J Biochem Biophys Methods. 2005 Dec 31;65(2-3):45-80.

Gomez-Abellan P, Hernandez-Morante JJ, Lujan JA, Madrid JA, Garaulet M. Clock genes are implicated in the human metabolic syndrome. Int J Obes. 2007 Jul 24.

Gomez-Abellan P, Hernandez-Morante JJ, Lujan JA, Madrid JA, Garaulet M. Clock genes are implicated in the human metabolic syndrome. Int J Obes. 2007 Jul 24.

González ME, Alarcón B, Carrasco L. Polysaccharides as antiviral agents: antiviral activity of carrageenan. Antimicrob Agents Chemother. 1987 Sep;31(9):1388-93.

Gould SJ. Eight Little Piggies. New York: Norton, 1993.

Gould SJ. Wonderful Life: The Burgess Shale and the nature of history. New York: Penguin Books, 1989.

Govindarajan VS, Sathyanarayana MN. Capsicum-production, technology, chemistry, and quality. Part V. Impact on physiology, pharmacology, nutrition, and metabolism; structure, pungency, pain, and desensitization sequences. Crit Rev Food Sci Nutr. 1991;29(6):435-74.

Govindarajan VS, Sathyanarayana MN. Capsicum-production, technology, chemistry, and quality. Part V. Impact on physiology, pharmacology, nutrition, and metabolism; structure, pungency, pain, and desensitization sequences. Crit Rev Food Sci Nutr. 1991;29(6):435-74.

Grad B, Dean E. Independent confirmation of infrared healer effects. In: White R, Broughton R (Eds.): Research in parapsychology 1983. Metuchen, NJ: Scarecrow Press, 1984:81-83.

Grad B. A Telekinetic Effect on Plant Growth. Intl Jnl Parapsy. 1964;6: 473.

Grad B. The 'Laying on of Hands': Implications for Psychotherapy, Gentling, and the Placebo Effect. Jnl Amer Soc for Psych Res. 1967 Oct;61(4): 286-305.

Grad, B. A telekinetic effect on plant growth: II. Experiments involving treatment of saline in stoppered bottles. Internl J Parapsychol. 1964;6:473-478, 484-488.

Grady D, Herrington D, Bittner V, Blumenthal R, Davidson M, Hlatky M, Hsia J, Hulley S, Herd A, Khan S, Newby LK, Waters D, Vittinghoff E, Wenger N. Cardiovascular disease outcomes during 6.8 years of hormone therapy: Heart and Estrogen/progestin Replacement Study follow-up (HERS II). JAMA. 2002 Jul 3;288(1):49-57.

Grasmuller S, Irnich D. Acupuncture in pain therapy. MMW Fortschr Med. 2007 Jun 21;149(25-26):37-9.

Grasso F, Grillo C, Musumeci F, Triglia A, Rodolico G, Cammisuli F, Rinzivillo C, Fragati G, Santuccio A, Rodolico M. Photon emission from normal and tumour human tissues. Experientia. 1992;48:10-13.

Grasso F, Musumeci F, Triglia A, Rodolico G, Cammisuli F, Rinzivillo C, Fragati G, Santuccio A, Rodolico M. In Stanley P, Kricka L (ed). Ultraweak Luminescence from Cancer Tissues. In Bioluminescence and Chemiluminescence—Current Status. New York: J Wiley & Sons. 1991:277-280.

Grasso F, Musumeci F, Triglia A. Yanbastiev M. Borisova, S. Self-irradiation effect on yeast cells. Photochemistry and Photobiology. 1991;54(1):147-149.

Grissom C. Magnetic field effects in biology: A survey of possible mechanisms with emphasis on radical pair recombination. Chem. Rev. 1995;95: 3-24.

Grobstein P. Directed movement in the frog: motor choice, spatial representation, free will? Neurobiology of motor programme selection. Pergamon Press, 1992.

Gupta YK, Gupta M, Kohli K. Neuroprotective role of melatonin in oxidative stress vulnerable brain. Indian J Physiol Pharmacol. 2003 Oct;47(4):373-86.

Gutmanis J. Hawaiian Herbal Medicine. Waipahu, HI: Island Heritage, 2001.

Haas M, Cooperstein R, Peterson D. Disentangling manual muscle testing and Applied Kinesiology: critique and reinterpretation of a literature review. Chiropr Osteopat. 2007 Aug 23;15:11.

Hagins WA, Penn RD, Yoshikami S. Dark current and photocurrent in retinal rods. Biophys J. 1970 May;10(5):380-412.

Hagins WA, Robinson WE, Yoshikami S. Ionic aspects of excitation in rod outer segments. Ciba Found Symp. 1975;(31):169-89.

Hagins WA, Yoshikami S. Ionic mechanisms in excitation of photoreceptors. Ann N Y Acad Sci. 1975 Dec 30;264:314-25.

Hagins WA, Yoshikami S. Proceedings: A role for Ca2+ in excitation of retinal rods and cones. Exp Eye Res. 1974 Mar;18(3):299-305.

Hagins WA. The visual process: Excitatory mechanisms in the primary receptor cells. Annu Rev Biophys Bioeng. 1972;1:131-58.

Halpern S. Tuning the Human Instrument. Palo Alto, CA: Spectrum Research Institute, 1978.

Hamel P. Through Music to the Self: How to Appreciate and Experience Music. Boulder: Shambala, 1979.

Hameroff SR, Penrose R. Conscious events as orchestrated spacetime selections. J Consc Studies. 1996;3(1):36-53.

Hameroff SR, Penrose R. Orchestrated reduction of quantum coherence in brain microtubules: A model for consciousness. In: Hameroff SN, Kaszniak A, Scott AC (eds.): Toward a Science of Consciousness— The First Tucson Discussions and Debates. Cambridge: MIT Press, 1996.

Hameroff SR, Smith, S, Watt.R. Nonlinear electrodynamics in cytoskeletal protein lattices. In: Adey W, Lawrence A (eds.), Nonlinear Electrodynamics in Biological Systems. 1984:567-583.

Hameroff SR, Watt, R. Information processing in microtubules. J Theor Biology. 1982;98:549-561.

Hameroff SR. Coherence in the cytoskeleton: Implications for biological information processing. In: Fröh- lich H. (ed.): Biological Coherence and Response to External Stimuli. Springer, Berlin-New York 1988, pp.242-264.

Hameroff SR. Light is heavy: Wave mechanics in proteins—A microtubule hologram model of conscious- ness. Proceedings 2nd. International Congress on Psychotronic Research. Monte Carlo, 1975:168-169.

Hameroff SR. Ultimate Biocomputing—Biomolecular Consciousness and Nanotechnology. Amsterdam: Elsevier, 1987.

Hamilton-Miller JM. Probiotics and prebiotics in the elderly. London: Department of Medical Microbiology, Royal Free and University College Medical School, 2004.

Handwerk B. Lobsters Navigate by Magnetism, Study Says. Natl Geogr News. 2003 Jan 6.

Hans J. The Structure and Dynamics of Waves and Vibrations. New York:.Schocken and Co., 1975.

Harlow HF, Dodsworth RO, Harlow MK. Total social isolation in monkeys. Proc Natl Acad Sci U S A. 1965.

Harlow HF. Development of affection in primates. In Bliss E (ed): Roots of Behavior. New York: Harper, 1962: 157-166.

Harlow HF. Early social deprivation and later behavior in the monkey. In: Abrams A, Gurner H, Tomal J (eds): Unfinished tasks in the behavioral sciences. Baltimore: Williams & Wilkins. 1964: 154-173.

Heart Disease. New York State Department of Health. Oct. 2004.

Hill N. Think and Grow Rich. Ralston Publishing, 1937, 1953.

Hillecke T, Nickel A, Bolay HV. Scientific perspectives on music therapy. Ann N Y Acad Sci. 2005 Dec;1060:271-82.

Hollfoth K. Effect of color therapy on health and wellbeing: colors are more than just physics. Pflege Z. 2000 Feb;53(2):111-2.

Hollwich F, Dieckhues B. Effect of light on the eye on metabolism and hormones. Klinische Monatsblatter fur Augenheilkunde. 1989;195(5):284-90.

Hollwich F. Hartmann C. Influence of light through the eyes on metabolism and hormones. Ophtalmologie. 1990;4(4):385-9.

Hollwich F. The influence of ocular light perception on metabolism in man and in animal. New York: Springer-Verlag, 1979.

Hope M. The Psychology of Healing. Longmead UK: Element Books, 1989.

Hu FB, Willett WC. Optimal diets for prevention of coronary heart disease. JAMA. 2002 Nov 27;288(20):2569-78.

Hu X, Wu B, Wang P. Displaying of meridian courses travelling over human body surface under natural conditions. Zhen Ci Yan Jiu. 1993;18(2):83-9.

Huang D, Ou B, Prior RL. The chemistry behind antioxidant capacity assays. J Agric Food Chem. 2005 Mar 23;53(6):1841-56.

Huffman C. Archytas of Tarentum: Pythagorean, philosopher and Mathematician King. Cambridge: Cam- bridge University Press, 2005.

Hull D. Science as a Process: An evolutionary account of the social and conceptual development of science. Chicago: Univ Chicago Press, 1988.

Hunt V. Infinite Mind: Science of the Human Vibrations of Consciousness. Malibu: Malibu Publ. 2000.

Hur YM, Rushton JP. Genetic and environmental contributions to prosocial behaviour in 2- to 9-year-old South Korean twins. Biol Lett. 2007 Aug 28.

Jahn R, Dunne, B. Margins of Reality: the Role of Consciousness in the Physical World. New York: Har- court Brace Jovanovich, 1987.

Johari H. Chakras. Rochester, VT: Destiny, 1987.

Johnston A. A spatial property of the retino-cortical mapping. Spatial Vision. 1986;1(4):319-331.

Johnston RE. Pheromones, the vomeronasal system, and communication. From hormonal responses to individual recognition. Ann N Y Acad Sci. 1998 Nov 30;855:333-48.

Kalmijn S, Launer LJ, Ott A, Witteman JC, Hofman A, Breteler MM. Dietary fat intake and the risk of incident dementia in the Rotterdam Study. Ann of Neurol. 1997;42(5):776-782.

Karnstedt J. Ions and Consciousness. Whole Self. 1991 Spring.

Keil J, Stevenson I. Do cases of the reincarnation type show similar features over many years? A study of Turkish cases. J. Sci. Exploration. 1999;13(2) 189-198.

REFERENCES AND BIBLIOGRAPHY

Keil J. New cases in Burma, Thailand, and Turkey: A limited field study replication of some aspects of Ian Stevenson's work. J. Sci. Exploration. 1991;5(1):27-59.

Kelder P. Ancient Secret of the Fountain of Youth: Book 1. New York: Doubleday, 1998.

Kerr CC, Rennie CJ, Robinson PA. Physiology-based modeling of cortical auditory evoked potentials. Biol Cybern. 2008 Feb;98(2):171-84.

Kirlian SD, Kirlian V, Photography and Visual Observation by Means of High-Frequency Currents. J Sci Appl Photog. 1963;6(6).

Klein E, Smith D, Laxminarayan R. Trends in Hospitalizations and Deaths in the United States Associated with Infections Caused by Staphylococcus aureus and MRSA, 1999-2004. Emerging Infectious Diseases. University of Florida Press Release. 2007 Dec 3.

Kobayashi M, Shoji N, Ohizumi Y. Gingerol, a novel cardiotonic agent, activates the Ca2+-pumping ATPase in skeletal and cardiac sarcoplasmic reticulum. Biochim Biophys Acta. 1987 Sep 18;903(1):96-102.

Koch C. Debunking the Digital Brain. Sci. Am. 1997 Feb.

Krebs K. The spiritual aspect of caring—an integral part of health and healing. Nurs Adm Q. 2001 Spring;25(3):55-60.

Kreig M. Black Market Medicine. New York: Bantam, 1968.

Kubler-Ross E. On Life After Death. Berkeley, CA: Celestial Arts, 1991.

Kumar PU, Adhikari P, Pereira P, Bhat P. Safety and efficacy of Hartone in stable angina pectoris-an open comparative trial. J Assoc Physicians India. 1999 Jul;47(7):685-9.

Kuuler R, Ballal S, Laike T Mikellides B, Tonello G. The impact of light and colour on psychological mood: a cross-cultral study of indoor work environments. Ergonomics. 2006 Nov 15;49(14):1496.

Lad V. Ayurveda: The Science of Self-Healing. Twin Lakes, WI: Lotus Press.

Lad V. Ayurveda: The Science of Self-Healing. Twin Lakes, WI: Lotus Press.

Lafrenière, G. The material Universe is made purely out of Aether. Matter is made of Waves. 2002. http://www.glafreniere.com/matter.htm. Acc. 2007 June.

Lakin-Thomas PL. Transcriptional feedback oscillators: maybe, maybe not. J Biol Rhythms. 2006 Apr;21(2):83-92.

Langhinrichsen-Rohling J, Palarea RE, Cohen J, Rohling ML. Breaking up is hard to do: unwanted pursuit behaviors following the dissolution of a romantic relationship. Violence Vict. 2000 Spring;15(1):73-90.

Latour E. Functional electrostimulation and its using in neurorehabilitation. Ortop Traumatol Rehabil. 2006 Dec 29;8(6):593-601.

Leape L. Lucian Leape on patient safety in U.S. hospitals. Interview by Peter I Buerhaus. J Nurs Scholarsh. 2004;36(4):366-70.

Lipkind M. Can the vitalistic Entelechia principle be a working instrument ? (The theory of the biological field of Alexander G.Gurvich). In: Popp F, Li K, Gu Q (eds.). Recent Advances in Biophoton Research. Singapore: World Sci Publ, 1992:469-494.

Lloyd D and Murray D. Redox rhythmicity: clocks at the core of temporal coherence. BioEssays. 2007;29(5): 465-473.

Lloyd JU. American Materia Medica, Therapeutics and Pharmacognosy. Portland, OR: Eclectic Medical Publications, 1989-1983.

Lucas WB (ed). Regression Therapy: A Handbook for Professionals. Past-Life Therapy. Crest Park, CA: Deep Forest Press, 1993.

Lydic R, Schoene WC, Czeisler CA, Moore-Ede MC. Suprachiasmatic region of the human hypothalamus: homolog to the primate circadian pacemaker? Sleep. 1980;2(3):355-61.

Lynch M, Walsh B. Genetics and Analysis of Quantitative Traits. Sunderland, MA: Sinauer, 1998

Lythgoe JN. Visual pigments and environmental light. Vision Res. 1984;24(11):1539-50.

Maccabee PJ, Amassian VE, Cracco RQ, Cracco JB, Eberle L, Rudell A. Stimulation of the human nervous system using the magnetic coil. J Clin Neurophysiol. 1991 Jan;8(1):38-55.

MacDougall D. The Soul: Hypothesis Concerning Soul Substance Together with Experimental Evidence of The Existence of Such Substance. J Am Soc Psych Res. 1907 May.

MacKay D. Science, Chance, and Providence. Oxford Univ Press, 1978.

MacKay D. The Open Mind and Other Essays. Downer's Grove, IL: Inter-Varsity Press, 1988.

Maes HH, Silberg JL, Neale MC, Eaves LJ. Genetic and cultural transmission of antisocial behavior: an extended twin parent model. Twin Res Hum Genet. 2007 Feb;10(1):136-50.

Makrides M, Neumann M, Byard R, Simmer K, Gibson R. Fatty acid composition of brain, retina, and erythrocytes in breast- and formula-fed infants. Am J Clin Nutr. 1994;60:189-94.

Mandino O. The Greatest Salesman in the World. Bantam 1968.

Mansour HA, Monk TH, Nimgaonkar VL. Circadian genes and bipolar disorder. Ann Med. 2005;37(3):196-205.

Marks C. Commissurotomy, Consciousness, and Unity of Mind. Cambridge: MIT Press, 1981.

Marks L. The Unity of the Senses: Interrelations among the Modalities. New York: Academic Press, 1978.

Mastorakos G, Pavlatou M. Exercise as a stress model and the interplay between the hypothalamus-pituitary-adrenal and the hypothalamus-pituitary-thyroid axes. Horm Metab Res. 2005 Sep;37(9):577-84.

Matutinovic Z, Galic M. Relative magnetic hearing threshold. Laryngol Rhinol Otol. 1982 Jan;61(1):38-41.

Maurer HR. Bromelain: biochemistry, pharmacology and medical use. Cell Mol Life Sci. 2001 Aug;58(9):1234-45.

Mayr E. Toward a New Philosophy of Biology: Observations of an evolutionist. Boston: Belknap Press, 1988.

McCauley B. 2005. Achieving Great Health. Spartan, Lansing, MI.

McTaggart L. The Field. New York: Quill, 2003.

Meinecke FW. Sequelae and rehabilitation of spinal cord injuries. Curr Opin Neurol Neurosurg. 1991 Oct;4(5):714-9.

Melzack R, Coderre TJ, Katz J, Vaccarino AL. Central neuroplasticity and pathological pain. Ann N Y Acad Sci. 2001 Mar;933:157-74.

Melzack R, Wall PD. Pain mechanisms: a new theory. Science. 1965 Nov 19;150(699):971-9.

Melzack R. Evolution of the neuromatrix theory of pain. The prithvi raj lecture: presented at the third world congress of world institute of pain, barcelona 2004. Pain Pract. 2005 Jun;5(2):85-94.

Melzack R. Pain: past, present and future. Can J Exp Psychol. 1993 Dec;47(4):615-29.

Melzack R. Pain—an overview. Acta Anaesthesiol Scand. 1999 Oct;43(9):880-4.

Miller GT. Living in the Environment. Belmont, CA: Wadsworth, 1996.

Miller K. Cholesterol and In-Hospital Mortality in Elderly Patients. Am Family Phys. 2004 May.

Mills A. A replication study: Three cases of children in northern India who are said to remember a previous life," J. Sci. Explor. 1989;3(2):133-184.

Mills A. Moslem cases of the reincarnation type in northern India: A test of the hypothesis of imposed identification, Part I: Analysis of 26 cases. J. Sci. Exploration. 1990;4(2):171-188.

Mindell E, Hopkins V. Prescription Alternatives. New Canaan CT: Keats, 1998.

Mishkin M, Appenzeller T. The Anatomy of Memory. Sci. Am. 1987 June.

Mishkin M. Memory in monkeys severely impaired by combined but not by separate removal of amygdala and hippocampus. Nature. 1978;273: 297-298.

Mitchell JL. Out-of-Body Experiences: A Handbook. New York: Ballantine Books, 1981.

Modern Biology. Austin: Harcourt Brace, 1993.

Monod J. Chance and Necessity. New York: Vintage, 1972.

Monroe R. Far Journeys. Garden City, NY: Doubleday & Co., 1985.

Monroe R. Journeys Out of the Body. Garden City, NY: Anchor Press, 1977.

Montanes P, Goldblum MC, Boller F. The naming impairment of living and nonliving items in Alzheimer's disease. J Int Neuropsychol Soc. 1995 Jan;1(1):39-48.

Moody R. Coming Back: A Psychiatrist Explores Past-Life Journeys. New York: Bantam Books, 1991.

Moody R. Life After Life. New York: Bantam, 1975.

Moody, R. Reflections on Lfe After Life: More Important Discoveries In The Ongoing Investigation Of Survival Of Life After Bodily Death. New York: Bantam, 1977.

Moore RY. Neural control of the pineal gland. Behav Brain Res. 1996;73(1-2):125-30.

Morick H. Introduction to the Philosophy of Mind: Readings from Descartes to Strawson. Glenview, Ill: Scott Foresman, 1970.

Morse M. Closer to the Light. New York: Ivy Books, 1990.

Motoyama H. Acupuncture Meridians. Science & Medicine. 1999 July/August.

Motoyama H. Before Polarization Current and the Acupuncture Meridians. Journal of Holistic Medicine. 1986;8(1&2).

Mumby DG, Wood ER, Pinel J. Object-recognition memory is only mildly impaired in rats with lesions of the hippocampus and amygdala. Psychobio. 1992;20: 18-27.

Municino A, Nicolino A, Milanese M, Gronda E, Andreuzzi B, Oliva F, Chiarella F, Cardio-HKT Study Group. Hydrotherapy in advanced heart failure: the cardio-HKT pilot study. Monaldi Arch Chest Dis. 2006 Dec;66(4):247-54.

Murchie G. The Seven Mysteries of Life. Boston: Houghton Mifflin Company, 1978.

Murray M and Pizzorno J. Encyclopedia of Natural Medicine. 2nd Edition. Roseville, CA: Prima Publishing, 1998.

Myss C. Anatomy of the Spirit. New York: Harmony, 1996.

Nakamura K, Urayama K, Hoshino Y. Lumbar cerebrospinal fluid pulse wave rising from pulsations of both the spinal cord and the brain in humans. Spinal Cord. 1997 Nov;35(11):735-9.

Nakatani K, Yau KW. Calcium and light adaptation in retinal rods and cones. Nature. 1988 Jul 7;334(6177):69-71.

Navarro Silvera SA, Rohan TE. Trace elements and cancer risk: a review of the epidemiologic evidence. Cancer Causes Control. 2007 Feb;18(1):7-27.

Nestel PJ. Adulthood—prevention: Cardiovascular disease. Med J Aust. 2002 Jun 3;176(11 Suppl):S118-9.

Nestor PJ, Graham KS, Bozeat S, Simons JS, Hodges JR. Memory consolidation and the hippocampus: further evidence from studies of autobiographical memory in semantic dementia and frontal variant frontotemporal dementia. Neuropsychologia. 2002;40(6):633-54.

Netheron M. Past Lives Therapy. New York: Morrow, 1978.Wambach H. Reliving Past Lives. New York: Bantam, 1978.Fiore E. You Have Been Here Before. New York: Ballantine, 1978.

Newton M. Destiny of Souls: New Case Studies of Life between Lives. St. Paul: Llewellyn Publications, 2000.

Newton M. Journey of Souls: Case Studies of Life between Lives. St. Paul: Llewellyn Publications, 1994.

Newton PE. The Effect of Sound on Plant Grwoth. JAES. 1971 Mar;19(3): 202-205.

Nishigori C, Hattori Y, Toyokuni S. Role of reactive oxygen species in skin carcinogenesis. Antioxid Redox Signal. 2004 Jun;6(3):561-70.

North J. The Fontana History of Astronomy and Cosmology. London: Fontana Press, 1994.

O'Dwyer JJ. College Physics. Pacific Grove, CA: Brooks/Cole, 1990.

O'Connell OF, Ryan L, O'Brien N. Xanthophyll carotenoids are more bioaccessible from fruits than dark green vegetables. Nutr Res. 2007;27(5):258-264.

Oehme FW (ed.). Toxicity of heavy metals in the environment. Part 1. New York: M.Dekker, 1979.

Ole D. Rughede, On the Theory and Physics of the Aether. Progress in Physics. 2006; (1).

O'Leary KD, Rosenbaum A, Hughes PC. Fluorescent lighting: a purported source of hyperactive behavior. J Abnorm Child Psychol. 1978 Sep;6(3):285-9.

Olney JW, Farber NB, Spitznagel E, Robins LN. Increasing brain tumor rates: is there a link to aspartame? J Neuropathol Exp Neurol. 1996;55:1115-23.

Olney JW. Excitotoxins in foods. Neurotoxicology. 1994;15:535-44.

Onder G, Landi F, Volpato S, Fellin R, Carbonin P, Gambassi G, Bernabei R. Serum cholesterol levels and in-hospital mortality in the elderly. Am J Med. 2003 Sept;115:265-71

One Hundred Million Americans See Medical Mistakes Directly Touching Them as Patients, Friends, Relatives. National Patient Safety Foundation. Press Release. 1997 Oct 9. http://npsf.org/pr/pressrel/finalsur.htm. Acc. 2007 Mar.

Oosterga M, ten Vaarwerk IA, DeJongste MJ, Staal MJ. Spinal cord stimulation in refractory angina pectoris—clinical results and mechanisms. Z Kardiol. 1997;86 Suppl 1:107-13.

Ostrander S, Schroeder L, Ostrander N. Super-Learning. New York: Delta, 1979.

Otani S. Memory trace in prefrontal cortex: theory for the cognitive switch. Biol Rev Camb Philos Soc. 2002 Nov;77(4):563-77.

Ott J. Color and Light: Their Effects on Plants, Animals, and People (Series of seven articles in seven issues). Internl J Biosoc Res. 1985-1991.

Ott J. Health and Light: The Effects of Natural and Artificial Light on Man and Other Living Things. Self published, 1973,

Pasricha S. Cases of the reincarnation type in northern India with birthmarks and birth defects. J. Sci. Exploration. 1998;12(2) 259-293.

Pasricha S. Claims of reincarnation: An Empirical Study of Cases in India. New Delhi: Harman, 1990.

Penn RD, Hagins WA. Kinetics of the photocurrent of retinal rods. Biophys J. 1972 Aug;12(8):1073-94.

Penn RD, Hagins WA. Signal transmission along retinal rods and the origin of the electroretinographic a-wave. Nature. 1969 Jul 12;223(5202):201-4.

Penson RT, Kyriakou H, Zuckerman D, Chabner BA, Lynch TJ Jr. Teams: communication in multidisciplinary care. Oncologist. 2006 May;11(5):520-6.

Perry J. A Dialogue on Personal Identity and Immortality. Indianapolis, IN: Hackett, 1978.

Perry J. Personal Identity. Berkeley: University of California Press, 1975.

Persinger M.A., Krippner S. Dream ESP experiments and geomagnetic activity. Journal of the American Society of Psychical Research. 1989;83:101- 106.

Persson R, Orbaek P, Kecklund G, Akerstedt T. Impact of an 84-hour workweek on biomarkers for stress, metabolic processes and diurnal rhythm. Scand J Work Environ Health. 2006 Oct;32(5):349-58.

Pert C. Molecules of Emotion. New York: Scribner, 1997.

Piluso LG, Moffatt-Smith C. Disinfection using ultraviolet radiation as an antimicrobial agent: a review and synthesis of mechanisms and concerns. PDA J Pharm Sci Technol. 2006 Jan-Feb;60(1):1-16.

Piolino P, Desgranges B, Belliard S, Matuszewski V, Lalevee C, De la Sayette V, Eustache F. Autobiographical memory and autonoetic consciousness: triple dissociation in neurodegenerative diseases. Brain. 2003 Oct;126(Pt 10):2203-19.

Piper PW. Yeast superoxide dismutase mutants reveal a pro-oxidant action of weak organic acid food preservatives. Free Radic Biol Med. 1999 Dec;27(11-12):1219-27.

Plotkin H. Darwin Machines and the Nature of Knowledge: Concerning adaptations, instinct and the evolution of intelligence. New York: Penguin, 1994.

Polkinghorne J. Science and Providence. Boston: Shambhala Publications, 1989.

Popp F, Chang J, Herzog A, Yan Z, Yan Y. Evidence of non-classical (squeezed) light in biological systems. Physics Lett. 2002;293:98-102.

Popp F, Yan Y. Delayed luminescence of biological systems in terms of coherent states. Phys.Lett. 2000;293:91-97.

Popp F. Molecular Aspects of Carcinogenesis. In Deutsch E, Moser K, Rainer H, Stacher A (eds.). Molecular Base of Malignancy. Stuttgart: G.Thieme, 1976:47-55.

Popp F. Properties of biophotons and their theoretical implications. Indian J Exper Biology. 2003 May;41:391-402.

Popper KR, Eccles, JC. The Self and Its Brain. London: Routledge, 1983.

Prescott J. Alienation of Affection. Psych Today. 1979 Dec.

Prescott J. The Origins of Human Love and Violence. Pre- and Perinatal Psych J. 1996;10(3):143-188.

Pribram K. Brain and perception: holonomy and structure in figural processing. Hillsdale, N. J.: Lawrence Erlbaum Assoc., 1991.

Protheroe WM, Captiotti ER, Newsom GH. Exploring the Universe. Columbus, OH: Merrill, 1989,

Puthoff H, Targ R, May E. Experimental Psi Research: Implication for Physics. AAAS Proceedings of the 1979 Symposium on the Role of Consciousness in the Physical World. 1981.

Puthoff H, Targ R. A Perceptual Channel for Information Transfer Over Kilometer distances: Historical Perspective and Recent Research. Proc. IEEE. 1976;64(3):329-254.

Radin D. The Conscious Universe. San Francisco: HarperEdge, 1997.

Raloff J. Ill Winds. Science News: 2001;160(14):218.

Rappoport J. Both sides of the pharmaceutical death coin. Townsend Letter for Doctors and Patients. 2006 Oct.

Rawlings M. Beyond Death's Door. New York: Bantam, 1979.

Reger D, Goode S, Mercer E. Chemistry: Principles & Practice. Fort Worth, TX: Harcourt Brace, 1993.

Reiter RJ, Garcia JJ, Pie J. Oxidative toxicity in models of neurodegeneration: responses to melatonin. Restor Neurol Neurosci. 1998 Jun;12(2-3):135-42.

Retallack D. The Sound of Music and Plants. Marina Del Rey, CA: Devorss, 1973.

Richards R. Darwin and the Emergence of Evolutionary Theories of Mind and Behavior. Chicago: Univ Chicago Press, 1987.

Rieder M. Mission to Millboro. Nevada City, CA: Blue Dolphin, 1995.

Rieder M. Return to Millboro: The Reincarnation Drama Continues. Nevada City, CA: Blue Dolphin, 1995.

Ring K. Life at Death: A Scientific Investigation of the Near-Death Experience. New York: Quill, 1982.

Roach M. Stiff: The Curious Lives of Human Cadavers. New York: W.W. Norton, 2003.

Rodale R. Our Next Frontier. Emmaus, PA: Rodale, 1981.

Rosenlund M, Picciotto S, Forastiere F, Stafoggia M, Perucci CA. Traffic-related air pollution in relation to incidence and prognosis of coronary heart disease. Epidemiology. 2008 Jan;19(1):121-8.

Rosenthal N, Blehar M (Eds.). Seasonal affective disorders and phototherapy. New York: Guildford Press, 1989.

Routasalo P, Isola A. The right to touch and be touched. Nurs Ethics. 1996 Jun;3(2):165-76.

Roy M, Kirschbaum C, Steptoe A. Intraindividual variation in recent stress exposure as a moderator of cortisol and testosterone levels. Ann Behav Med. 2003 Dec;26(3):194-200.

Rubin E and Farber J. Pathology 3rd Edition. Lippincott-Raven, Philadelphia, PA, 1999.

Russ MJ, Clark WC, Cross LW, Kemperman I, Kakuma T, Harrison K. Pain and self-injury in borderline patients: sensory decision theory, coping strategies, and locus of control. Psychiatry Res. 1996 Jun 26;63(1):57-65.

Russek LG, Schwartz GE. Narrative descriptions of parental love and caring predict health status in midlife: a 35-year follow-up of the Harvard Mastery of Stress Study. Altern Ther Health Med. 1996 Nov;2(6):55-62.

Saarijarvi S, Lauerma H, Helenius H, Saarilehto S. Seasonal affective disorders among rural Finns and Lapps. Acta Psychiatr Scand. 1999 Feb;99(2):95-101.

Sabom M. Light and Death: One Doctor's Fascinating Account of Near Death Experiences. Grand Rapids, MI: Zondervan Publishing, 1998.

Sabom M. Recollections of Death: A Medical Investigation. New York: Harper and Row, 1982.

Sacks O. The Man Who Mistook his Wife for a Hat and Other Clinical Tales. New York: Simon & Schuster, 1998.

REFERENCES AND BIBLIOGRAPHY

Sanders R. Slow brain waves play key role in coordinating complex activity. UC Berkeley News. 2006 Sep 14.

Schlebusch KP, Maric-Oehler W, Popp FA. Biophotonics in the infrared spectral range reveal acupuncture meridian structure of the body. J Altern Complement Med. 2005 Feb;11(1):171-3.

Schmitt B, Frölich L. Creative therapy options for patients with dementia—a systematic review. Fortschr Neurol Psychiatr. 2007 Dec;75(12):699-707.

Scoville WB, Milner B. Loss of recent memory after bilateral hippocampal lesions. J Neurol Neurosurg Psychiatry. 1957;20:11-21.

Semenza C. Retrieval pathways for common and proper names. Cortex. 2006 Aug;42(6):884-91.

Senekowitsch F, Endler PC, Pongratz W, Smith CW. Hormone effects by CD record /replay. FASEB J. 1995:A12025.

Senior F. Fallout. New York Mag. 2003 Fall.

Serway R. Physicis For Scientists & Engineers. Philadelphia: Harcourt Brace, 1992.

Shaffer D. Developmental Psychology: Theory, Research and Applications. Monterey, CA: Brooks/Cole, 1985.

Shankar R. My Music, My Life. New York: Simon & Schuster, 1968.

Shapiro RN, Jordan G. Dare to Prepare: How to Win Before You Begin. Three Rivers, 2008.

Sharp KC. After the Light. New York: William Morrow & Co., 1995.

Shevelev IA, Kostelianetz NB, Kamenkovich VM, Sharaev GA. EEG alpha-wave in the visual cortex: check of the hypothesis of the scanning process. Int J Psychophysiol. 1991 Aug;11(2):195-201.

Shupak NM, Prato FS, Thomas AW. Human exposure to a specific pulsed magnetic field: effects on thermal sensory and pain thresholds. Neurosci Lett. 2004 Jun 10;363(2):157-62.

Skwerer RG, Jacobsen FM, Duncan CC, Kelly KA, Sack DA, Tamarkin L, Gaist PA, Kasper S, Rosenthal NE. Neurobiology of Seasonal Affective Disorder and Phototherapy. J Biolog Rhyth. 1988;3(2):135-154.

Sloan F and Gelband (ed). Cancer Control Opportunities in Low- and Middle-Income Countries. Committee on Cancer Control in Low- and Middle-Income Countries. 2007.

Smith CW. Coherence in living biological systems. Neural Network World. 1994:4(3):379-388.

Smith MJ. "Effect of Magnetic Fields on Enzyme Reactivity" in Barnothy M.(ed.), Biological Effects of Magnetic Fields. New York: Plenum Press, 1969.

Smith MJ. The Influence on Enzyme Growth By the 'Laying on of Hands: Dimensions of Healing. Los Altos, California: Academy of Parapsychology and Medicine, 1973.

Snyder K. Researchers Produce Firsts with Bursts of Light: Team generates most energetic terahertz pulses yet, observes useful optical phenomena. Press Release: Brookhaven National Laboratory. 2007 July 24.

Soul Has Weight, Physician Thinks. The New York Times. 1907 March 11:5.

Southgate, D. Nature and variability of human food consumption. Philosophical Transactions of the Royal Society of London. 1991;B(334): 281-288.

Spence A. Basic Human Anatomy. Menlo Park, CA: Benjamin/Commings, 1986.

Spetner L. Not By Chance! -Shattering The Modern Theory of Evolution. New York: The Judaica Press, 1997.

Spillane M. Good Vibrations, A Sound 'Diet' for Plants. The Growing Edge. 1991 Spring.

Squire LR, Zola-Morgan S. The medial temporal lobe memory system. Science. 1991;253(5026):1380-1386.

Steck B. Effects of optical radiation on man. Light Resch Techn. 1982;14:130-141.

Stevenson I, Samararatne G. Three new cases of the reincarnation type in Sri Lanka with written records made before verification. J. Sci. Exploration. 1988;2(2): 217-238.

Stevenson I. American children who claim to remember previous lives. J. Nervous and Mental Disease. 1983;171:742-748.

Stevenson I. Cases of the Reincarnation Type. Charlottesville, VA: Univ Virginia Press. Vol. 1: Ten Cases in India, 1975. Vol. 2: Ten Cases in Sri Lanka, 1977. Vol. 3: Twelve Cases in Lebanon and Turkey, 1980. Vol. 4: Twelve Cases in Thailand and Burma, 1983.

Stevenson I. Children Who Remember Previous Lives: A Question of Reincarnation. Charlottesville, VA: Univ Virginia Press, 1987.

Stevenson I. European Cases of the Reincarnation Type. Jefferson, NC: McFarland and Co., 2003.

Stevenson I. Reincarnation and Biology: A Contribution to the Etiology of Birthmarks and Birth Defects. (2 volumes). Westport, CN: Praeger Publishers, 1997.

Stevenson I. Twenty Cases Suggestive of Reincarnation. New York: American Society for Psychical Research, 1967.

Stevenson I. Where Reincarnation and Biology Intersect. Westport, CN: Praeger, 1997.

Stojanovic MP, Abdi S. Spinal cord stimulation. Pain Physician. 2002 Apr;5(2):156-66.

Stoupel E, Kalediene R, Petrauskiene J, Gaizauskiene A, Israelevich P, Abramson E, Sulkes J. Monthly number of newborns and environmental physical activity. Medicina Kaunas. 2006;42(3):238-41.

Strange BA, Dolan RJ. Anterior medial temporal lobe in human cognition: memory for fear and the unexpected. Cognit Neuropsychiatry. 2006 May;11(3):198-218.

Suppes P, Han B, Epelboim J, Lu ZL. Invariance of brain-wave representations of simple visual images and their names. Proc Natl Acad Sci Psych-BS. 1999;96(25):14658-14663.

Szyf M, McGowan P, Meaney MJ. The social environment and the epigenome. Environ Mol Mutagen. 2008 Jan;49(1):46-60.

Targ R, Katra J, Brown D, Wiegand W. Viewing the future: A pilot study with an error-detecting protocol. J Sci Expl. 9:3:367-380, 1995.

Targ R, Puthoff H. Information transfer under conditions of sensory shielding. Nature. 1975;251:602-607.

Taylor A. Soul Traveler: A Guide to Out-of-Body Experiences and the Wonders Beyond. New York: Penguin, 2000.

Thaut MH. The future of music in therapy and medicine. Ann N Y Acad Sci. 2005 Dec;1060:303-8.

The Mystery of Smell. Howard Hughes Medical Instit. http://www.hhmi.org/senses/d110.html. Acc. 2007 Jul.

The Timechart Company. Timetables of Medicine. New York: Black Dog & Leventhal, 2000.

Thie J. Touch for Health. Marina del Rey, CA: Devorss Publications, 1973-1994.

Thomas Y, Schiff M, Litime M, Belkadi L, Benveniste J. Direct transmission to cells of a molecular signal (phorbol myristate acetate, PMA) via an electronic device. FASEB Jnl. 1995;9: A227.

Thomas-Anterion C, Jacquin K, Laurent B. Differential mechanisms of impairment of remote memory in Alzheimer's and frontotemporal dementia. Dement Geriatr Cogn Disord. 2000 Mar-Apr;11(2):100-6.

Thompson D. On Growth and Form. Cambridge: Cambridge University Press, 1992.

Thorogood M, Mann J, Appleby P, McPherson K. Risk of death from cancer and ischaemic heart disease in meat and non-meat eaters. BMJ. 1994 June 25;308:1667-1670.

Threlkeld DS, ed. Central Nervous System Drugs, Analeptics, Caffeine. Facts and Comparisons Drug Information. St. Louis, MO: Facts and Comparisons. 1998 Feb: 230-d.

Threlkeld DS, ed. Gastrointestinal Drugs, Proton Pump Inhibitors. Facts and Comparisons Drug Information. St. Louis, MO: Facts and Comparisons. 1998 Apr: 305r.

Timofeev I, Steriade M. Low-frequency rhythms in the thalamus of intact-cortex and decorticated cats. J Neurophysiol. 1996 Dec;76(6):4152-68.

Tiwari M. Ayurveda: A Life of Balance. Rochester, VT: Healing Arts, 1995.

Tompkins, P, Bird C. The Secret Life of Plants. New York: Harper & Row, 1973.

Toomer G. "Ptolemy". The Dictionary of Scientific Biography. New York: Gale Cengage, 1970.

Triglia A, La Malfa G, Musumeci F, Leonardi C, Scordino A. Delayed luminsecence as an indicator of tomato fruit quality. J Food Sci. 1998;63:512-515.

Tucker J. Life Before Life: A Scientific Investigation of Children's Memories of Previous Lives. New York: St. Martin's Press, 2005.

Valgimigli L, Sapone A, Canistro D, Broccoli M, Gatta L, Soleti A, Paolini M. Oxidative stress and aging: a non-invasive EPR investigation in human volunteers. Aging Clin Exp Res. 2014 Jul 31.

Van Cauter E, Leproult R, Plat L. Age-related changes in slow wave sleep and REM sleep and relationship with growth hormone and cortisol levels in healthy men. JAMA. 2000 Aug 16;284(7):861-8.

Vargha-Khadem F, Polkey CE. A review of cognitive outcome after hemidecortication in humans. Adv Exp Med Biol. 1992;325:137-51.

Vescelius E. Music and Health. New York: Goodyear Book Shop, 1918.

Vickers A. Botanical medicines for the treatment of cancer: rationale, overview of current data, and methodological considerations for phase I and II trials. Cancer Invest. 2002;20(7-8):1069-79.

Vickers AJ, Kuo J, Cassileth BR. Unconventional anticancer agents: a systematic review of clinical trials. J Clin Oncol. 2006 Jan 1;24(1):136-40.

Walker M. The Power of Color. Gujarat, India: Jain Publ., 2002.

Watson L. Beyond Supernature. New York: Bantam, 1987.

Watson L. Supernature. New York: Bantam, 1973.

Wattles W. The Science of Getting Rich. Elizabeth Towne, 1910

Wayne R. Chemistry of the Atmospheres. Oxford Press, 1991.

Weaver J, Astumian R. The response of living cells to very weak electric fields: the thermal noise limit. Science. 1990;247: 459-462.

Wee K, Rogers T, Altan BS, Hackney SA, Hamm C. Engineering and medical applications of diatoms. J Nanosci Nanotechnol. 2005 Jan;5(1):88-91.

Weinberger P, Measures M. The effect of two audible sound frequencies on the germination and growth of a spring and winter wheat. Can. J. Bot. 1968;46(9):1151-1158.

Weiss B. Many Lives, Many Masters. New York: Simon & Schuster, 1988.

Westman M, Eden D. Effects of a respite from work on burnout: vacation relief and fade-out. J Appl Psychol. 1997 Aug;82(4):516-27.

Wetterberg L. Light and biological rhythms. J Intern Med. 1994 Jan;235(1):5-19.

White J, Krippner S (eds). Future Science: Life Energies & the Physics of Paranormal Phenomena. Garden City: Anchor, 1977.

White S. The Unity of the Self. Cambridge: MIT Press, 1991.

Whittaker E. History of the Theories of Aether and Electricity. New York: Nelson LTD, 1953.

Whitton J. Life Between Life. New York: Warner, 1986.

Williams G. Natural Selection: Domains, levels, and challenges. Oxford: Oxford Univ Press, 1992.

Winchester AM. Biology and its Relation to Mankind. New York: Van Nostrand Reinhold, 1969.

Wixted JT. A Theory About Why We Forget What We Once Knew. CurrDir Psychol Sci. 2005;14(1):6-9.

Wolf, M. Beyond the Point Particle—A Wave Structure for the Electron. Galilean Electrodynamics. 1995 Oct;6(5): 83-91.

Woolger R. Other Lives, Other Selves. New York: Bantam, 1988.

Zhang C, Popp, F., Bischof, M.(eds.). Electromagnetic standing waves as background of acupuncture system. Current Development in Biophysics—the Stage from an Ugly Duckling to a Beautiful Swan. Hangzhou: Hangzhou University Press, 1996.

Zizza, C. The nutrient content of the Italian food supply 1961-1992. European Journal of Clinical Nutrition. 1997;51: 259-265.

Zou Z, Li F, Buck L. Odor maps in the olfactory cortex. Proc Natl Acad of Sci. 2005;102(May 24):7724-7729.

Index

Manufactured by Amazon.ca
Acheson, AB

12906340R00113